More Country Walks

in Warwickshire and Worcestershire

A second collection by
Des Wright

Meridian Books

Published 1998 by Meridian Books

© Des Wright 1998

ISBN 1-869922-37-9

A catalogue record for this book is available from the British Library

Meridian Books
40 Hadzor Road, Oldbury, Warley, West Midlands B68 9LA

Printed in Great Britain by MFP Design & Print, Manchester

Contents

Introduction

"But walking isn't really a sport is it" said Jo Ind of the *Birmingham Post*. She was responding to my assertion, in *Country Walks in Warwickshire and Worcestershire* (hereafter referred to as *Country Walks*), that walking is probably the most popular participatory sport in this country. There followed a lengthy discussion as to how the word 'sport' should be defined.

- Has a sport to involve a competitive element? Then what of the lonely jogger or the person who regularly swims twenty lengths in the local swimming pool?

- Has it to involve physical exertion? Then what of chess players and anglers who use up very few extra calories.

- Could we class hobbies as sports? So do we include embroidery, gardening and choral singing?
...And so it went on and, in the absence of an all-embracing definition, we agreed to accept my original assertion and to classify walking as a sport.

Medical research has shown that walking produces the same short- and long-term benefits as any other sport but is less wearing on the joints than jogging or aerobics. But beware of the warning given by Nick Crane after an 18 month, 6,000 mile trek along the watershed of Europe: 'Walking turns you into a sort of stringy skeleton – your top half a coathanger for a rucksack, your legs all sinewy and muscular'. But, who cares? Most of us don't indulge in marathon walks like Nick does!

We walkers are fortunate. We have over 100,000 miles of public footpaths and bridleways on which we may practise our sport. We should pay tribute to those organisations, large and small, whose members strive to keep these rights of way open and who maintain their stiles, gates and footbridges. Good work is also being done in the provision of waymarks. In the text, I have generally omitted mention of these as some, often vital ones, become vandalised, are removed or are used as target practice. However, where they exist, they provide a reassuring bonus in route-finding. Walkers are also grateful to those who provide, in churchyards and on village greens, commemorative seats upon which we can rest weary limbs and take on energy-providing food and drink.

On occasions, the routes prescribed cross crop-bearing fields. If you feel uneasy about these, you may wish to walk around their perimeters. Indeed, if the crop is mature maize or rapeseed, you may have little choice for these can become quite impenetrable. However, where I have indicated a cross-field path, it follows the line of a right-of-way. Where cultivation occurs over a path, the law dictates that the footpath should be reinstated within two weeks. When this is done, walkers keep to the path and minimise crop-trampling, facilitating this by walking in single file. Where the law is ignored, it does not deter walkers but it increases damage to crops. This may be the place to remind those who walk in the countryside, particularly in the winter, that they must be prepared for mud so strong shoes or boots are essential.

I have written elsewhere about the acts of theft and vandalism which have led to the locking of so many of the country churches visited on these walks. However, on this theme, there is a story with a happy ending. On the cover of *Country Walks*, there is a photograph of the Three-Parish Sign, erected by Wythall Countryside Carers at the point where the boundaries of the parishes of Alvechurch, Beoley and Wythall meet. In the autumn of 1997, the sign mysteriously disappeared. It was later found, nailed to a stile in Wast Hills Lane, 2½ 'crow-miles' from its original site! You will be pleased to know that the kidnapped sign was recovered, complete and undamaged, and will soon be back in its rightful place.

I would like to thank those who have made constructive suggestions about the contents of *Country Walks* and I am also indebted to the following for useful information: Jim Andrew (Birmingham Museum of Science and Industry), Vivian Bird (for the account of Hall End Farm), Rev John Ganjavi (Ullenhall Church), Mr G. Goulding (Royal Warwickshire Regiment), Fred Hathway (Meriden/Berkswell), Roy Jamieson (British Waterways), Roy Pearson (Wythall Countryside Carers), David and Marcia Slater (for the Hadleigh story), the Highways Agency, the Institute of Terrestrial Ecology and the Ordnance Survey. The maps have again been carefully drawn by my son, Chris, and my wife, Pauline, has checked some of the walks and has shown considerable patience during this book's preparation. Finally, I am most grateful to Peter Groves, publisher of Meridian Books, who has personally checked all the walks (using public transport exclusively), has provided all but one of the photographs and has again been a valued source of advice and encouragement during the past few months.

Having spent the early years of my life in south Shropshire, it is not surprising that I have absorbed an enduring love of the countryside and a deep fascination of the creatures that inhabit it. Perhaps Edgar Brooks, in his *Country Rambles* (undated, but the price of ninepence – i.e. less than four new, post-decimal pence – gives a clue to its antiquity) sums up this attitude with these words:

'The value of woodland strolls does not simply consist in the amount of pure air we breathe, or of the exercise we take, valuable as these things are to our well-being. The truth so often re-iterated by wise men and women, that there is a higher culture and education to be derived from nature than from books, is no idle sentiment'.

I wish you well and hope that you enjoy these walks!

Des Wright
Kings Heath
Birmingham

Using this book

ALL the walks are circular, delivering you back to your car or, in most cases, to public transport. Where public transport is known to be available, brief details are given in the introductory box to each walk. However, changes are not uncommon so for up-to-date information and for news of new services and of old ones which have been withdrawn you should contact:

British Rail	0345-484950
Centro (West Midlands)	0121-200 2700
Warwickshire Transport Operations	01926-412135
Hereford and Worcester County Busline	01345-125436

The location of suitable car parks is given wherever possible; otherwise roadside parking is necessary. Where pub car parks are mentioned, landlords have been consulted. However, ownership may have changed so it would be courteous to ask their permission first and to make use of their refreshment facilities later.

At certain times of the year, mud abounds in the countryside and so boots or strong shoes are strongly recommended. Inevitably, parts of these walks are on public roads, some of them narrow. Please be careful! Also, if your dog is keen to enjoy a country walk with you, please ensure that it is kept under control and remember that not every walker is a dog-lover, many being terrified by the over-enthusiastic approaches of some of our canine friends! Several of the walks pass through sheep pastures and, in these circumstances, dogs must always be kept on a lead.

The sketch maps accompanying each walk are intended to serve as guidance and not as replacements for the appropriate Ordnance Survey maps. Even though you may not always need to use them OS maps are invaluable if in emergency, bad weather or other reason you wish to cut short or re-route your walk. The appropriate numbers of the Landranger (1:50,000) and Pathfinder (1:25,000, with much greater detail) are given in the introduction box at the start of each walk, where you will also find grid references (GR) for the starting and finishing points, together with other useful information. (If you are unsure about the grid reference system you will find this explained on the Ordnance Survey Landranger maps.)

It is always wise to carry a compass, a basic first aid kit and some food and drink. Secateurs can sometimes be useful.

Location Map

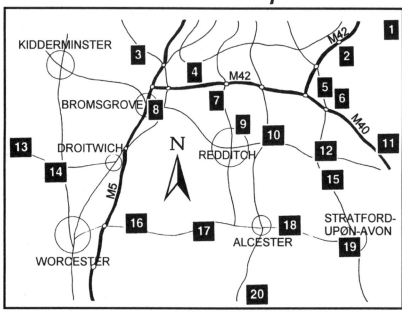

Publishers' Note

Every care has been taken in the preparation of this book. All the walks have been independently checked and are believed to be correct at the time of publication. However, no guarantee can be given that they contain no errors or omissions and neither the publishers nor the author can accept responsibility for loss, damage, injury or inconvenience resulting from the use of this book.

Please remember that the countryside is continually changing: hedges and fences may be removed or re-sited; footbridges and river banks may suffer from flood damage; landmarks may disappear; footpaths may be re-routed or ploughed over and not reinstated (as the law requires); concessionary paths may be closed. If you do encounter any such problems the publishers would be very pleased to have details. Obstructions to rights of way should always be reported to the appropriate local authority. These are:

Warwickshire:

Rights of Way Section
Planning and Transportation
 Department
Shire Hall
Warwick
CV34 4SX

Worcestershire:

Rights of Way Section
County Hall
Spetchley Road
Worcester
WR5 2NP

1
Exploring the Meriden Gap

This walk explores an interesting wedge of countryside which keeps apart the margins of two large cities and, en route, visits the pretty village of Berkswell.

Start: Church Lane, Meriden (GR250820)
Distance: 8 miles; shorter option 5½ miles.
Maps: Landranger 139 & 140; Pathfinder 935 & 955.
Parking: There is ample roadside parking in Church Lane, Meriden. This is off the B4102 road about three quarters of a mile east of Meriden town centre. N.B. Church Lane is a crescent, each end of which joins the B4102. The portion where the walk starts is the western arm of the crescent i.e. the one nearer to Meriden. (GR250820)
Public Transport: TWM bus service 900 runs between Birmingham and Coventry via Meriden and stops near Church Lane. N.B. See note above about Church Lane.
Some trains between Birmingham and Coventry stop at Berkswell Station (*longer walk only*). Leave the platform and turn left along Truggist Lane for about a quarter of a mile to join the main walk at ★ on page 4 (This will add half a mile to the walk (unless you omit the possible pub stop in Meriden.)
Refreshments: The Bear Inn, Berkswell and The Queen's Head, Meriden (150 yards along Old Road, just opposite your starting point). For rail travellers: The Railway, Berkswell Station (SW side of the station).

WALK up Church Lane from the B4102 and, at the top of the incline where the lane swings left, ignore the path leading off to the right and take the footpath straight ahead. Hedge removal has made this field very long. On a well-trodden path, walk initially across the field and then, continuing by a hedge, proceed to the field's end. Here, cross a stile and walk on with the hedge at your left hand. After crossing the next stile (just through the hedge, beside a gate), bear half left and walk to the top left-hand corner of the next field.

Here cross a stile and proceed up a slight incline with the hedge on your left. At the next stile, continue up the gentle slope a quarter left, aiming for a clump of trees on the horizon. Reaching the trees, cross a stile and walk with the trees, now revealed as the end of an old hedge composed mainly of hawthorn, blackthorn and crab-apple, at your left hand. Continue through this paddock, the hedge soon being replaced by a wooden fence.

As you walk through this paddock, you can see, in the distance to your right, the centre of Birmingham and, to your left, tall buildings on the west side of Coventry. This much-cherished piece of green-belt land is ever under threat from the expansion of the two cities. However, the importance of this 'Meriden Gap' as a belt of relatively unspoilt countryside is overwhelming.

Leave the paddock via a stile and walk down a gravelled drive to reach a roadway (Back Lane). Cross this and the stile opposite and walk on with the hedge still on your left for about 150 yards. At a field corner (which originally,

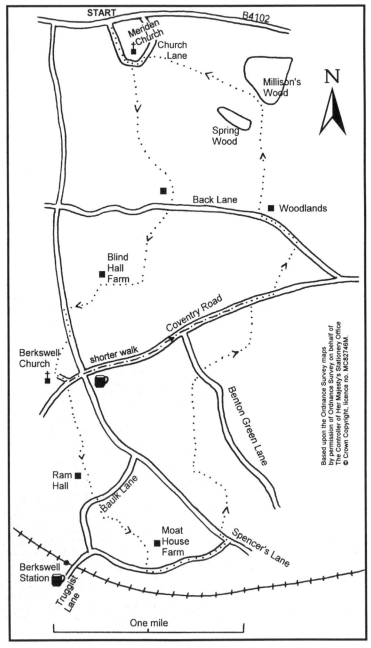

2

before hedge removal, was at the end of the field), notice a shady pool on your left. Immediately after this follow the path as its swings briefly to the right and then, under a large oak, resumes its former heading as it enters the next field. Now walk on through this, and two more fields with the hedge, intermittent at times, at your right hand.

When you come to the marshy corner of the third field, ignore the waymarked stile on your right and follow the hedge as it swings left and then right. At a farm gate, turn sharp right in front of a house. You are now on a farm track the surface of which improves after you pass through a wicket gate alongside a cattle grid. Walk on down the incline, passing in front of the pretty, timber-framed Blind Hall Farm. When the lane joins the Meriden-Berkswell road, turn left.

Use the tarmacked pavement to walk on for about 300 yards. Passing the road sign which indicates your imminent arrival in Berkswell (a sign surrounded, in spring, by a mass of golden daffodils), and shortly before a speed restriction sign, carefully cross the road to pass through a kissing gate and follow a clear path which leads to Berkswell church with a good view of Berkswell Hall across fields to the right. Enter the well-maintained churchyard via a kissing gate on its north side.

To attempt adequately to describe the Church of St John the Baptist, Berkswell in a few lines would be insulting. It is a gem amongst country churches with its crypts, Norman arches, imposing stepped nave, barrel-roofed chancel with ornately-carved choir stalls, and many other noteworthy features. You will, no doubt, wish to spend time here using, to explain the history of this marvellous building, the informative guidebook available in the church.

As you leave the main (south) door of the church, the house immediately ahead of you (over the wall) was once the home of Maud Watson, the first Ladies' Singles Champion at Wimbledon in 1884. Turn left and, shortly before leaving the churchyard, visit a small, open-sided chapel which commemorates those who died in warfare during the twentieth century.

The magnificent entrance porch to the Church of St John the Baptist, Berkswell

Passing through the main gates, notice, immediately on your right, the village well. Walk on down Church Lane, passing the village school on your left, to reach the village green. Here there is an oak tree planted at the time of the Queen's Coronation in 1953, a set of wooden stocks with five holes – to accommodate three malefactors, one of whom had a wooden leg, so the story goes! – and several seats on which to rest awhile.

The longer and shorter walks separate here. For the longer walk continue reading from ○ below.

Following the **shorter** walk continue to the end of Church Lane where it joins Lavender Hall Lane and continue along this road to the cross roads. Here, go ahead into Coventry Road and walk along this for nearly a mile to rejoin the main walk at ✿ on page 5)

○ The next path for the **longer** walk is easily missed. As you stand on the village green with your back to the Post Office, look across Lavender Hall Road and your path is just to the right of a house called Copper Beeches. You have now parted company with the Heart of England Way which you have followed from Meriden so will no longer be reassured by its distinctive waymarks. However, the traditional yellow waymarks are reasonably abundant throughout the remainder of the walk.

Entering the path by Copper Beeches and passing under a brick archway belonging to the neighbouring house, walk in a more-or-less southerly direction with the hedge on your right. (The area around the second stile can, after heavy rain in winter, be *very* muddy.) 100 yards after the third stile, cross a stile in the hedge and immediately resume your former heading, now with the hedge at your left side.

Continue to the bottom of the field where you turn right for 40 yards and, shortly after passing a cattle trough, cross a stile on your left (in the shadow of a huge oak) and walk up an incline towards Ram Hall (built in about 1600). At the top, pass through the first gate, go to the left of the second one, and then cross over a stile on your right. Walk on, with the old sandstone farmhouse on your right, to join a farm road which leads down to a lane (Baulk Lane).

Cross this lane and, slightly to the left of a pool, climb over a stile. The clear path goes straight down the field passing close to a stout electricity post. Beneath a gnarled old oak, cross the first of two plank bridges and immediately turn left and follow the field boundary initially by a ditch and then, swinging right, through two fields by a well-trimmed hedge. When you reach the first large oak tree, take a path diagonally to your right across the field, aiming just to the right of an electricity pylon. Here bear right onto a rough lane and, passing beside Moat House Farm, walk on and turn left onto a road (Truggist Lane).

★ *If you have travelled by train, leave or meet the longer walk here.*

Walk on down Truggist Lane (passing Hodgetts Lane on your right) and finally turn left into the main road (Spencer's Lane). Carefully cross this and, immediately beyond a house called Byways, cross a stile on the right. Walk with the hedge initially on your right, then swing very slightly right (keeping to the right of the first electricity post) to cross a small concrete footbridge. Continuing on the same bearing, cross the field to reach and go through a gap into the next field. Now walk on, with the tall hedge on the right, soon passing over a stream by way of a bridge composed of several old railway sleepers.

About 125 yards beyond this rough bridge, you will see a stile on your right. *Do not cross this*, but turn 90° to your left and walk to an overgrown hedge. Follow this hedge and subsequent fence (you may soon wish to skirt well to the left of a small, *very boggy* area) and cross the next stile. Just before the end of the next field, cross a stile on the right and choose the path which goes straight ahead with the hedge on your right. Continue until, just less than 100 yards before overhead electricity wires, you see a stile on your right, continuing on the Coventry Way. Cross this, turn left and continue on your former heading with the hedge now on your left.

When this hedge abruptly goes off to the left, bear slightly right to join an indistinct path which leads in the direction of the (left hand) white house. (More hedges have been grubbed out here and so the paths are, at present, less conspicuous.) When you get to within about 30 yards of the white house, you turn right onto a well-trodden path which leads to a stile by a large tree stump. Cross this stile and walk down a tarmacked lane to a road (Benton Green Lane).

Surveys of U.K. hedgerows by the Institute of Terrestrial Ecology reveal a 33% decrease from 1984 to 1993. However, the rate of removal has steadily declined during this period and from 1990 to 1993, more hedges were replanted than grubbed up. This may reflect changes in financial inducements, grant-aid for removal being gradually phased out and replaced by subsidies for replanting. However, it will take years for the new hedges to achieve the biological diversity of those ancient structures which had stood for centuries.

Turn left into Benton Green Road for a few yards and, just past the red-brick Benton Green Farmhouse, turn right through a gap and walk on with the hedge on your right. Pass through a metal field gate and go straight on, across two fields. At the end of the second field, just before a large gap, take a stile on the left beneath an ash tree. Walk on with the meandering hedge on your right. When you come to a stile in the hedge, cross it and turn immediately left.

Continue through a scrubby paddock, now with the hedge on the left. Just as you begin to think that there is no way ahead, you will see a waymarked stile to the left of tall cupressus trees. Pass along this enclosed path noticing the foxgloves which will be in flower in summer. When you cross the next stile, you will be surprised (and, maybe, embarrassed!) to be in someone's back garden. Walk ahead on this right of way, close to the hedge on your left, and pass the end of the house to reach the road (Coventry Road) into which you turn right.

✿ *The shorter walk meets the main route here.*

Walk on for about 200 yards and, where Coventry Road changes to Broad Lane, cross a stile on the left. Walk on for 30 yards and go through the gate in front of you, ignoring the stile leading off to the right. The line of the path may not now be clear but, as you stand with your back to the gate, ignore the pylon in the field ahead but aim for a stile on the horizon between the next two pylons to the right.

Cross this stile and, maintaining the same heading, walk across the next field (noting its strong ridge-and-furrow pattern) aiming just to the right of a pair of trees which stand in front on white houses. Cross a stile to reach a road onto which you turn left. Walk on, initially passing the entrance to a farm shop and then, a little further on, passing Shirley Lane and a group of houses on your right. Just beyond a red-brick redevelopment called Woodlands, cross a stile on the right and walk ahead with the brick buildings on your right.

Follow a tractor track which soon goes left and then right. Continue on this and, 100 yards after a prominent dead oak, the hedge peters out but you continue on the track across a field to a spinney. When you reach this, turn right and then, in 20 yards, turn left and cross two stiles separated by a footbridge and walk along the eastern edge of Spring Wood.

At the end of the spinney, walk ahead to another, larger, patch of woodland (Millison's Wood) and when you reach it, make a 90° turn to the left. The edge of the woodland soon goes off to the right but you stay on the same heading as you walk up to the top of the field where you cross a stile beside a gate. As you proceed, with the hedge on your right, the tower of Meriden church comes into view The path develops into a tractor track and soon passes beside large lumps of rock and concrete.

The surface of these stones has become colonised by mosses and yellow and grey lichens. Lichens are complex, being a partnership between two sets of organisms. Fungi anchor the lichen to the stone and protect the other partners, algae, which, like ordinary plants, use sunlight to make food by photosynthesis. They are good pollution indicators being very susceptible to sulphurous gases in the atmosphere. And one other point – the litmus that you use(d) in chemistry lessons at school is derived from lichens!

Approaching the brow of the hill, cross another stile and, with the hedge now on your left, approach Moat House Farm (the second farm of that name that you have seen today, this one dated 1609, but probably much older). Just before the start of the extended farmyard (complete with its bales of straw and discarded farm machinery) bear half right across the field aiming for a gateway beside which a stile leads to Church Lane. Turn left into the lane and soon enter the churchyard by a gate.

St Lawrence's Church was founded by a missionary sent by Lady Godiva nearly a thousand years ago. Sadly, it is generally padlocked on weekdays.

Leaving the churchyard by the main gate, turn right and pass, in front of Church Farm, staddle stones (which would have formerly supported a granary to exclude rodents) and a stone mounting platform (where lady riders would have mounted or dismounted from their horses). Walk on down Church Lane.

If you have travelled by train, you have a choice here. If you want some refreshment, you can continue along the lane as it swings right and down to the main road. The Queen's Head is the just along Old Road, opposite. However, if you prefer to go straight back to Berkswell Station then, just before the lane swings to the right, take a path on the left and follow the instructions from the beginning of the walk.

If using car or bus follow the lane as it swings to the right and leads back to your starting point.

2
Knowle and Barston

Start: Knowle church (GR182767).
Maps: Landranger 139; Pathfinder 954 & 955.
Distance: 8 miles; shorter option 6 miles
Parking: Use of free car parks in Knowle (the most convenient is in St John's Close) is limited to three hours except on Sundays and Bank Holidays, but there is car parking on roadsides nearby.
Public Transport: TWM bus service 38 (Solihull/Dorridge). (*Service 40, Solihull/Knowle, takes a longer route than the 38.*)
Refreshments: Pubs and coffee shops in Knowle, The Bull's Head in Barston, The Black Boy on the canal-side (if using the longer route).

FROM the church and the neighbouring Guildhall (1412), walk away from the village down Kenilworth Road soon noticing, on your left, an interesting row of cottages variously decorated with carved tiles and diapered brickwork, one commemorating Queen Victoria's Jubilee in 1897 – Jubilee House. Take the first turn on your left and enter Kixley Lane and soon pass a relatively unusual National Trust property, a recreation ground called Knowle Children's Field. Houses stretch on down the road and, about 80 yards beyond the last house on the left (number 59), cross a stile on the left.

Ignore the footbridge ahead and bear half right to a stile in the hedge. Cross this and turn left to follow a well-trodden path round the perimeter of the field. At the end of the field, cross the Grand Union Canal via a tall bridge, dated 1913, and, at the bottom of the steps on the far side, turn right and walk on along the towpath with the canal on your left.

Just before the first road bridge (number 73), take a path which slants up to the right to reach the road onto which you turn right. This is a busy stretch but you stay on it for only 40 yards before you turn right into the drive of Waterfield Farm. Walk on past a tall, neatly-cut evergreen hedge on your left, pass through field gates and continue between brick buildings soon to reach a broad, hedge-lined tractor track. Follow this forward: just beyond an electricity pylon, it does a abrupt left-right turn to pass to the left side of Nappins Covert. This, in season, is carpeted with bluebells and also houses a rookery, the raucous cries of its inhabitants being much in evidence during the nesting period.

The five members of the crow family most commonly seen in the two counties are jackdaws, jays, magpies, rooks and carrion crows. Whereas rooks nest communally, have a white base to their beaks and have feathered thighs which give them a 'baggy trousers' look, crows are solitary nesters, their beaks are completely black and they are sleeker than rooks.

Soon after passing a large, roofless, red-brick barn (still complete with its cast-iron water pump), pass through a wide gateway and immediately turn left. In 25 yards, pass a redundant stile and take a clear path half right across the field, an oak and an ash forming your guard-of-honour as you approach the far corner. Crossing the subsequent stile, follow a path diagonally right across the next field which delivers you to a concrete footbridge. Use this to cross the River Blythe and having done so, turn left to walk round the field margin to a stile into a lane.

Cross the lane and, slightly to the left, climb over a stile into a field. Your next objective is a stile half-left up the incline. It is between two trees which are just to the right of a red-brick house with three dormer windows. Having negotiated this stile, continue on the same heading to the left field corner

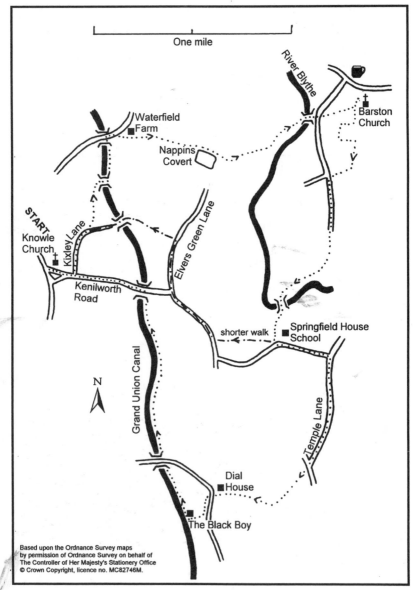

where, just beyond a barn, you cross another stile to enter the churchyard of St Swithin's, Barston.

Having walked around the attractively wooded churchyard leave it the same way as you entered but, instead of slanting off to the right after crossing the stile, continue ahead, walking down an incline with a tall hedge at you left hand. At the bottom of the slope, turn right and proceed now with paddock rails on your left. At the end of the paddock rails, cross two stiles on your left and then, on the same heading, cross two more (the first overgrown but with a gate on the left) to reach a driveway.

Turn left onto this and, as the driveway swings to the left, go through a gate ahead of you. Walk on for 60 yards until, just before an ornamental pool complete with waterlilies and footbridge, cross a stile on your right. Walk up the meadow aiming slightly to the right of the leftmost of two electricity pylons that you can see ahead, to reach a stile. Cross this (which in the event turns out to be a treble one) and then bear three-quarters right to walk across a long, narrow field to find a stile alongside the metal gates and railings of Barston Park.

Turn left to pass Elvers Green Lane and walk up a metalled 'No Through Road' to its end some 600 yards ahead. Here cross two stiles in close proximity and then follow a track which curves gently off to the right with the fence at your left side. Ahead of you is Springfield House School around which you will soon be walking. At the next stile, the fence changes sides. Soon after passing a gnarled old oak which has probably stood on its solitary sentry duty for several centuries, the path bears to the left to cross an old iron-railed, stone bridge by way of which you again cross the River Blythe. At the other side, bear sharp right to a kissing gate leading into a spinney through which your clear path meanders between clumps of comfrey.

Exploring the folk lore of Britain's wild plants, Richard Mabey, in his enchanting book 'Flora Britannica', writes of the comfrey, a plant so beloved of herbalists from medieval times to the present day. He vividly describes the range of uses to which

Bridge over the River Blythe

the plant has been put, from healing of flesh wounds, through re-growth of bone fractures (common names of the plant include 'knit-bone' and 'bone-set') to relief of arthritis. However, take professional advice before using it!

Emerging from the spinney, the path leads you to the right round the perimeter of the school's building and finally reaches a tarmac drive into which you turn right. In 60 yards, just before the end of the drive, you will see a waymarked stile on your right.

Here, the two walks separate. For the shorter walk continue with the following paragraph. For the longer walk continue from ★ below.

Cross this stile and walk through this long field with the hedge on your right. On reaching a road, turn right and walk along its nearside pavement to the first intersection. Here, turn right into Elvers Green Lane. Just before Elvers Green Farm, cross a stile on the left and walk, with the hedge on your left, to the next stile. Cross this and walk on a short distance to cross a plank bridge. A few yards ahead is the final stile of your walk. Having squeezed through this, soon lower your head to pass under a large fallen willow tree to reach a lane (Kixley Lane) which leads you over the canal and, ultimately, to Kenilworth Road into which you turn right to reach your starting point.

★ Continuing with the **longer** route turn your back on the stile and take a short path opposite, through trees to reach a road. Turn left and pass the entrance to Springfield House School. Cross the very busy B4101 soon after the school (to avoid having to make an awkward crossing later) and walk on down the incline making use where possible of the narrow grass verge and, preferably, walking in single file. Cross the River Blythe once again and when the road swings off to the left, turn right into the much-quieter Temple Lane. You soon pass the cemetery's sandstone lych-gate which commemorates those who died in two World Wars.

If you enter the cemetery and walk to its far left corner, you will see a gravestone which records the death, in 1924, of Henry James Williams who wrote the song "It's a long way to Tipperary".

At the end of Temple Lane, turn left into Chadwick Lane, leaving behind the quaintly-named Cuttle Pool Lane. In 30 yards, join a tarmac drive on the right and, walking to the right of a house called Park Corner, enter a waymarked, enclosed footpath. At the end of this, pass through a kissing gate to reach a cart track onto which you turn right. 100 yards after crossing a stream, carry straight ahead through a wooden gate which leads to another enclosed path which soon veers off to the left to skirt the garden of a delightful, timber-framed house the walls of which are decorated with wistaria flowers in summer. This house is called The Dial House – look for the sundial on one of its chimneys. When you reach a road, cross it and turn left to walk on its broad verge until, as the road veers away to the left, you walk up the metalled drive of the Black Boy.

The Black Boy dates back to 1793. Pubs of this name are said to commemorate Charles II who, apparently, had dark skin and raven-black hair.

A path just to the left of the pub buildings leads to the towpath of the Grand Union Canal onto which you turn right. Walk on, passing a plethora of moored boats of various shapes and sizes. At bridge 70 you pass the Heronfield Animal Rescue Centre ('Please come in and look around'). Soon the splendid Knowle Locks come into view – a flight of five locks, each separated by a broad pool. Originally there were six narrow locks here but they were replaced by the present five wide locks when the Grand Union was modernised in the 1930s. You can see the remains of some of the old locks in the side-weirs. Knowle Church can be seen half-left reminding you that your objective is not far away.

Having passed boatyards beyond the top lock, take a track to the right just before you reach a road bridge (number 71). On reaching the road (Kenilworth Road), turn left (noting the old weighbridge at the side of the road where goods would have been weighed before being loaded onto boats at Knowle Hall Wharf, now the boatyard) and walk back to your starting point.

Knowle's splendid church is a noble spot at which to end your walk, one of its many interesting features being an hour glass above the pulpit for the timing of sermons! The neighbouring Guild House was built in the fifteenth century by Walter Cook as the original headquarters of the Guild of St Anne.

3
Explorations Around Belbroughton

The intricate network of paths in this area allows you to explore some delightful, quiet countryside via undulating paths and to visit Harvington Hall.

Start: Belbroughton (GR919769)
Distance: 9 miles; shorter option 6 miles.
Maps: Landranger 139; Pathfinder 953.
Parking: Roadsides on Church Road near Holy Trinity Church, Belbroughton. Motorists start reading from ★ *on page 13.*
Public Transport: Midland Red West service 318 (Stourbridge/Bromsgrove). Alight at The Talbot, Belbroughton.
Refreshments: The Talbot, The Queens and The Olde Horseshoe in Belbroughton. The Moatside Restaurant at Harvington Hall (open Tues, Wed, Thurs, Sun (Mar-Oct).
Special Feature: Harvington Hall. *For opening times, telephone 01562 777846.*

IF you have arrived by bus from Stourbridge, cross the road from the Talbot and turn right (if arriving from Bromsgrove walk forward), turn left along High Street to pass the village green. On this you will see an old scythe works hammer and nearby, on the wall, a plaque recording the transportation to Australia in 1787 of Sarah Bellamy, a Belbroughton resident convicted of theft. Turn left at the junction into Church Road.

Hammer from old scythe works, now on the village green

★ Walk up nearly to the top of Church Road noting, bulging through the churchyard wall, a gigantic sweet chestnut tree.

Sweet chestnut trees are thought to have been introduced from Italy into Britain by the Romans – it is known that, on mainland Europe, the Roman army was fed on flour made from the nuts. The tree can be long-lived. The age of this specimen is

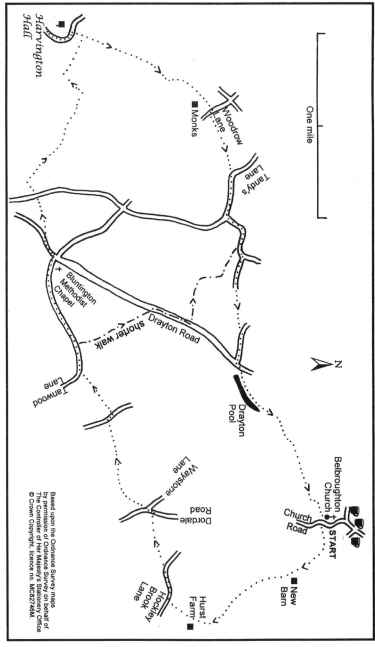

not known as there is no record of its planting but it is mentioned in local histories in 1850 and in 1883 when it was said to be 'upwards of seventeen feet in circumference'. That measurement now exceeds 25 feet.

In the churchyard you will see an ancient cross, restored in memory of a soldier killed during the Boer War at Spion Kop in 1900.

Opposite the church is Belbroughton First School. Just to the left of the school join a clear, surfaced footpath which leads away from Church Road and soon passes beside gardens and allotments to reach a tarmac drive serving a leisure centre. Turn right here and proceed with the leisure centre building close at your left hand. Having walked straight on alongside a playing field, cross a stile and continue with the hedge still at your right-hand side. Having crossed the next stile, your well-trodden path takes you straight across a field to another stile.

Cross this and then climb a short incline to reach a grassy area containing the walls of a stone and brick barn ('New Barn' on the OS map.). Walk anticlockwise around this and cross, at its far side, another stile which leads to a downhill path. Near the bottom of the slope, the path veers slightly left to another stile. Beyond this you pass up another gentle incline to cross a stile which is well-shaded by trees.

Now continue ahead with intermittent oaks at your right hand. Just after the last of these oaks (the seventh, and the weakest!), continue with a hedge at your left side to pass, in about 100 yards, through a hedge gap. Follow the path as it veers slightly to the right and walk up a field in the direction of a white farmhouse (Hurst Farm). Follow the track with the farmhouse and outbuildings on your left, having ignored a waymarked stile near the farmhouse. On a clear day you will have ahead (W) a view of the distant Malvern Hills. Just beyond the outbuildings, you swing left to join a rough lane onto which you turn right. At the end of this lane, you reach Hockley Brook Lane into which you turn right.

Walk on, passing Rose Cottage on your right, having ignored a public bridleway immediately before it. After about 200 yards, the lane turns abruptly to the right. 30 yards after this bend, take a stile on your left and, leaving the barns on your left side, go slightly left (W) down a slight incline and pass through a gateway to the left of a field corner. (*There is another gateway further to the right. This is not the one you want.*) Now aim for a stile in the hedge at the opposite side of the field and having crossed this, walk up the field ahead and climb over a stile which is just in front of a white house.

Turn left onto Dordale Road and, in about 50 yards, reach its junction with Waystone Lane. Immediately cross Waystone Lane to your path which is between two houses, just to the left of a red-brick gate pillar. This path is narrow and may look rather uninviting. At its end, you reach a field. Here, turn right and follow the boundary hedge for 50 yards where it turns sharply left and then, in another 60 yards, sharply right. (Be alert here for the next stile is very easily missed.) Ten yards or so after this right turn, divert slightly right and follow an indistinct (and somewhat overgrown) path as it descends with a hedge still at your right hand to a stile, which you cross.

Continue down the slope aiming for metal farm gates to the right-hand side of a large pool. Having negotiated these two barriers, walk to your next stile which is in the far right hand corner of the next paddock. Cross this and, with the hedge on your right hand side, walk on (ignoring a stile on the right after some 25 yards), crossing another stile, a (*possibly temporary*) gate and then another stile, to reach a roadway into which you turn right.

In about 50 yards, just before the far end of a spinney, turn left and pass through the spinney to emerge into a field along the right-hand margin of which you walk onwards with the slender spire of Chaddesley Corbett church now in view directly ahead.

On clear days, a fine panorama has been opening out before you with, slightly to the right of the church spire, the Abberley Hills, half-left (and just to the right of Chaddesley Woods visited on Walk 3 in 'Country Walks') the jagged outline of the Malverns. On the far right the Clee Hills are just coming into view.

Emerging onto a road (Tanwood Lane) via a stile in the corner of the field, turn right and walk on past the sun-dialled Tanwood House.

About 100 yards beyond Tanwood House, the two routes diverge. For the longer route continue reading from ✿ *below.*

Continuing the **shorter** route turn right into a signposted bridleway, soon ignoring another bridleway which goes off to the right after about 50 yards. Follow the waymarked path which is just to the left of the gateway to a large garden. This enclosed path soon emerges into a field onto which you immediately turn right. Follow the hedge as it soon swings to the left and ascends a slope, accompanied overhead by triple electricity cables.

Just beyond the top of the incline, at the field's end, go through a gap in the hedge and, turning half left, use a diagonal path to cross the next field. On reaching a roadway (Drayton Road), turn right and use the grass verge to walk over the brow of the hill and down the slope on the other side, noting the Clent Hills ahead of you.

Near the bottom of the incline, turn left onto a marked path (signposted Hill Pool) and follow the tarmacked track up a gentle slope. Just after the track begins to descend, walk up to a stile on your left beneath a twin-forked oak tree and, having crossed this, follow the boundary on your right as it begins its gentle descent towards Hill Pool, crossing a stile beside a gate *en route.*

Gorse bushes are abundant on the slopes here. The fact that the bushes are rarely without their yellow flowers has given rise to the saying: "When gorse is in blossom, kissing's in season".

At the bottom of the hill, cross two stiles and a footbridge, walk up a short path to a concrete drive into which you turn right, rejoining the longer route at ✿ on page 17.

✿ Following the **longer** route continue along Tanwood Lane for about half a mile into Bluntington village. A little over 100 yards after passing the Methodist Chapel (built in 1873), you reach a crossroads and take the road on your left (sign-posted Chaddesley Corbett). In about 200 yards, you come to a 30 mile-an-hour sign and soon after this, the road swings off to the left. You cross the road carefully here and continue ahead on the same bearing, keeping the boundary of this large rhubarb field on your left-hand side.

At the end of the field, pass between two short, concrete posts and walk down steps to use a house driveway to reach a road (being reassured, by a signpost on the verge outside, that you have indeed used a right-of-way!). Cross the road and continue on a drive opposite, passing 'Green Acres'. You are now on the Monarch's Way, a long-distance path which links Worcester with Charmouth on the south coast. In 100 yards, you reach a gate. Do *not* pass through it but turn right to follow the well-trodden path up the incline, just to the right of an electricity post, when the Clees may again be visible ahead. Walk down the slope to a rough farm track which takes you on down the slope and through a gate.

Walk on, with the hedge on your right. After 150 yards, climb an easily overlooked stile on your right and continue, on your former heading, but now with the hedge/fence on your left. Continue ahead even when the hedge disappears for 120 yards or so. After the gap, walk on, with the hedge now on your right, to pass through a hedge gap.

Turn left onto a farm track which leads you round the perimeter of a large field, performing a right-angle bend *en route*. Ignore a lane which soon goes off to your left towards farm buildings, continuing with the red earth beneath your feet for a further 200 yards or so. When the track veers abruptly to the left, follow it for about 100 yards to a roadway into which you turn left. Walk on to Harvington Hall, passing the Hall's moat and a very large tree stump on your way.

Harvington Hall stands on a moated island which was made about 1260. Parts of the Hall are medieval, but most of it was built by Humphrey Pakington about 1580. It is well-known for its priest-holes in which Roman Catholic priests evaded persecution in the sixteenth and seventeenth centuries. John Wall, one of the last Roman Catholics to die for his faith in England, may well have been captured here.

Retrace your steps back along the roadway and turn right to rejoin the red-earth track you used earlier. After about 100 yards, ignore the right turn by which you came, and walk straight ahead with the hedge on your right, soon passing at intervals maple trees which, in late summer, have beautiful, reddish-purple leaves. At the field's end, walk ahead through a gap and proceed with a hedge now on your left and ignore a waymarked path going off to the left in a couple of hundred yards.

Soon after the hedge starts to swing off to the left, look out directly ahead for the white-painted walls and chimneys of a house ('Monks', which you will pass later). 50 yards after this house comes into view (you may have seen the tops of its chimneys a little way back), cross a stile just off to your left through a gap in the hedge. From the stile, go half left across a paddock (in the direction of another white-walled house) and then follow waymarks to reach a pair of stiles on the right. These lead to a short, enclosed path on which it is wise to beware of hidden rabbit burrows.

At the end of this path, negotiate a stile and then continue on your former bearing with the wire boundary now on your right. The Clent Hills can soon be seen ahead of you with 'Monks' on your right. When you come to a road (Woodrow Lane), turn right onto it and, in 60 yards, turn into a semi-tarmacked lane on your left. Ignoring a private drive which veers off to the left (to Frere Felde), continue ahead with the hedge on your left, soon walking under an electricity pylon which stands astride the path. Cross a stile and at the end of the hedge, cross another stile and then go half-right of your former heading(E), noticing the abundant fairy rings as you walk across the field to a stile which leads into a lane (Tandy's Lane).

Turn right into Tandy's Lane and follow it as it swings sharply to the left and climbs gently to reach a road T-junction. Here you turn left onto a narrow road leading to Hill Pool. Follow this as it descends into the village, noticing as you reach the village the exposed sandstone rock faces from which the red earth of the area is derived. At the bottom of the incline, having entered the village, the road veers left. Immediately after crossing a bridge over a babbling stream, turn right into a rough lane. (This is easily missed, so be alert here.) In 50 yards or so, the surface changes to concrete and it is at this point that the shorter route rejoins the longer one.

✿ *The stream which walkers of the longer route have just crossed, and will accompany us for the next mile or so, is the Belne Brook which, on its journey down through Belbroughton and Drayton, was an important source of water power from the sixteenth century. It was of particular significance to the scythe-making industry which was centred on this area from the late 1700s until just after World War II.*

In a few yards, cross a stile on the left and go straight up a short incline to cross another stile on the horizon. Turn right to cross another stile and keep the field boundary (and the stream beyond it) at your right hand, watching out for badger setts which can provide an unsuspected hazard in the path. Continue for about a quarter of a mile until a road is reached, beside a bungalow. Here turn right and, at the next T-junction, cross the road and turn left (signposted Belbroughton and Stourbridge).

Just beyond a small business complex (Drayton Mill) cross a stile beside a gate to enter a gravelled area leading to a large pool (Drayton Pool). Walk on with the pool initially on your right and, after about a quarter of a mile, use a footbridge to cross the stream. At the other side, turn left and walk through trees

past derelict factory buildings to emerge onto a roughly tarmacked area. Here, bear right and follow the track past a water-treatment unit. Beyond the works, continue your ascent, the slender fourteenth century spire of Belbroughton church coming into view at the brow of the hill. Walk down, through a gate, and, just before the next gate, turn left and, in a few paces, take an enclosed path which leads into the churchyard to complete the walk.

The Domesday Book records that there was a church in Belbroughton in Saxon times. Though generally locked during the week, a notice on its door shows that the present Holy Trinity Church, can be entered and admired by borrowing the key from the Rectory. It has many interesting features, all well-described in literature available within the church.

Cross in Belbroughton Churchyard

17

4
Barnt Green, Reservoirs and a Country Park

On this short walk, on the very edge of the West Midlands conurbation, town and country are starkly contrasted.

Start: Barnt Green (GR 008737)
Distance: 4½ miles.
Maps: Landranger 139; Pathfinder 953 & 954.
Parking: Roadsides in Hewell Road, Barnt Green (but beware of parking restrictions!).
Public Transport: Travel West Midland service number 145 (between Birmingham and Bromsgrove, *not Sundays*) calls at Barnt Green station. Trains between Lichfield and Redditch stop at Barnt Green station. Leave the station from the platform 4 exit and walk through the car park and along Station Approach.
Refreshments: The Visitor Centre on the Lickey Hills and, in Barnt Green, tea rooms and The Victoria pub.

THE walk starts at the junction of Hewell Road and Station Approach in Barnt Green. With your back to the station, turn left, walk down Hewell Road and, at its end, turn right into Bittell Road. Continue ahead for 100 yards and turn left and walk down Margesson Drive. At the bottom, 10 yards beyond a prominent oak tree, pass through a gap in a tall, evergreen hedge (signed Bittell Farm Road) and enter the car park of Barnt Green Sports Club.

Go to the right of the buildings and, just beyond the last of them (and when you thought there was no way ahead!), turn left and, in 10 yards, go over a stile on your right. With a holly hedge on your left, walk down a playing field at the bottom of which, just beyond young trees sporting their protective collars, you cross a stile. Walk on with the hedge on your left, soon passing a muddy gateway.

At the end of this field, cross a stile and go half-right on a well-used path which passes close to a tree-fringed pool. On reaching a road, turn left and walk on for nearly 20 yards to join a bridleway (signed Cofton Church). As you walk up this lane, you pass to the left of the Mill Shrub, a shady pool much-loved by birds and ornithologists alike. Continue on the bridleway for nearly half-a-mile and stay on it as it swings right just before a pool. Then continue straight ahead over a stile beside which is a five-trunked silver birch tree, its branches liberally decorated with warty growths. Walk up an incline for nearly 100 yards to reach Upper Bittell Reservoir. Now used by fishing and sailing clubs, Upper Bittell is also an important water bird refuge, particularly in the winter. As you go, you, pass a large, bricked-up building.

Mill Shrub

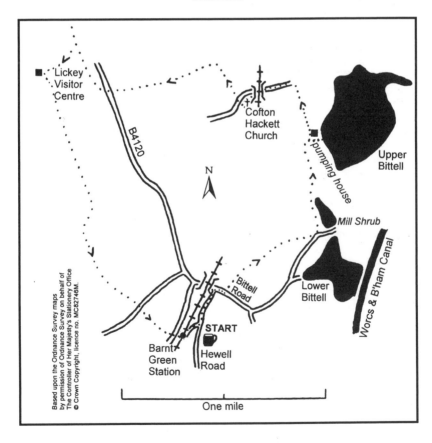

This used to house a large steam engine which was designed by Boulton, Watt and Co., built at Soho foundry and installed in 1837 at a cost of £3,270. Its 64 inch diameter cylinder was capable of pumping water, which had overflowed from the Worcester and Birmingham Canal into Lower Bittell reservoir, into Upper Bittell, lifting it 54 feet in the process.

Retrace your steps back down the slope, climb the stile and turn right. Walk on, passing two quiet pools and the delightful Tower House. When you reach a T-junction, turn left and walk ahead, still on the North Worcestershire Path, soon to pass under a railway. 20 yards beyond the bridge, go up a set of stone steps on your left to enter the graveyard of St. Michael's Church, Cofton Hackett.

Once, no doubt, a quiet, country church, St Michael's is waiting to be swallowed up by the spreading city. For reasons of security, you may not be able to get any further than its fine old porch, the timbers of which date from the fifteenth century. The bell cote, with its two bells, is also fifteenth century. The remains of the church cross, probably dating back to the fourteenth century, can be seen near to the entrance.

Leave the church by a path going west and, just before holly bushes, notice the grave of Alfred John 'Jackie' Draper, a 17-year-old victim of enemy action in 1940, no doubt the result of an air-raid. The nearby Austin works, then engaged in producing aircraft (including 300 Hurricanes and 330 Lancaster bombers) and aircraft components, was of great strategic importance at that time.

Continue past the holly bushes to rejoin the lane. Here, turn left and, in 80 yards, climb a stile on your right and walk up the slope with the field boundary on your right. Near the top of the rise, turn left and continue your ascent to cross a tarmacked path by way of two stiles. Walk on, with a rough wire fence initially at your right hand, until you cross a stile at the far end of the field, this stile being just to the right of a house with five dormer windows

Remains of the old cross in Cofton Hackett church

20

The 'Spirit of the Woods' Sculpture on the Lickey Hills

and a white gable-end. Walk on along an enclosed path which soon merges with a drive which leads up to a road.

Cross this carefully and, by way of a clear path opposite, begin your assault on the Lickey Hills. Immediately after a flight of log-supported steps, turn right onto a bridleway. As you continue your ascent, notice the green-stemmed bilberry bushes alongside you – you are climbing Bilberry Hill. At a car park at the top, bear right onto a gravel path, passing a dew pond on your right, soon to reach a viewing platform which reminds you of the proximity of town and country in this area and on which plaques help you to identify landmarks near and far. Just beyond this pass another dew pond, then turn left along a broad path. As this approaches the car park go to the right of a group of trees to pass the car park on your left and reach a road. Turn right along this to reach the Visitor Centre on your left.

The Visitor Centre was opened in 1990 and may provide a useful resting place now that you have done nearly all your climbing for the day. Light refreshments are available but the spot may be over-populated on fine weekends, particularly in the warmer months.

From the main doors and terrace on the south side of the Visitor Centre, go straight down steps and onto a path which leads to the left of a fenced-off children's playground.

Beyond the playground, in a grassy area on the right, you will see a wooden sculpture. This is called 'Spirit of the Woods' and was carved out of a sweet chestnut log by Graham Jones in 1993 and is one of a collection of such works to be found in this woodland. (Details in the Visitor Centre.)

From the sculpture, walk back to the track and continue on its gentle incline, ignoring another track which goes off to the left at the end of the stand of tall, Scots pines. 100 yards after a wooden shelter, swing right by wooden palings and begin to climb gently. Stay on this track, the muddy parts of which are easily circumnavigated, as it swings off to the left and begins its descent towards the village of Barnt Green, passing another wooden shelter *en route*. In their flowering seasons, you will see isolated clumps of wild daffodils ('Lent lilies') and abundant bluebells beside you as you go. On reaching a road, turn left and in 10 yards take a path on the right through further woodland.

During your walk through the woods, you will probably have seen grey squirrels. This species, introduced to this country from North American the late 1800s, is one which we either love or hate. It can be looked upon as a charming addition to our fauna or as a destructive pest – a 'rat with a bushy tail'. We take our pick!

Walk down a pleasant avenue of beeches to reach a road. Cross the railway line by way of the bridge a little to your left, walk through the car park and down Station Approach to your starting place. For refreshment turn right to tea rooms and the Victoria pub (200 yds.).

5
Hockley Heath and a Mysterious Obelisk

A walk which contrasts the modern with the more traditional modes of transport.

Start: The War Memorial near a petrol station on the A3400 at the south end of Hockley Heath (GR153726).
Distance: 7 miles; shorter option 5½ miles.
Parking: Roadsides off the A3400 in Hockley Heath.
Maps: Landranger 139; Pathfinder 954.
Public Transport: Stagecoach service X50 between Birmingham, Stratford-on-Avon and Oxford stops in Hockley Heath.
Refreshments: The Wharf Tavern and the Nag's Head (Hockley Heath).

A FTER viewing the memorial, which carries an interesting three-faced sundial, cross the road to the Wharf Tavern. Walk south, over the canal bridge and turn right into Spring Lane using the near-side pavement. Continue as the road swings right by St Thomas' Church and passes the premises of a steam engine enthusiast. When the pavement ends, cross *with the greatest care* to that which starts opposite. Continue for just under 100 yards where, just *beyond* Umberslade Manse and where the pavement ends, you turn left to walk up a long drive towards Umberslade Baptist Church.

At the top of the drive, pass a derelict wooden chapel before walking anticlockwise round the church to the far left-hand corner of its burial ground to a stile. Cross this and the next one and bear just to the right of the large barn ahead. A stile leads to an enclosed path which passes yet another, long-abandoned place of worship, now used to shelter farm animals. Though some of the leaning tombstones surrounding it date from the 1850s, the most recent one was put up in 1995. Continue past the old church to a lane, the stile opposite leading to an obelisk, conspicuous from the nearby motorway.

Many travellers speeding past must wonder what this structure commemorates.

Sundial on the War Memorial

23

It bears no inscription and, in consequence, several myths have circulated about its origin. The most likely explanation concerns Thomas Archer, who lived at Umberslade Hall and who, incidentally, was the architect of St Philip's Cathedral in Birmingham. It is said that he built the obelisk in 1747 to celebrate his elevation to the House of Lords.

Having examined the obelisk, return to the lane, turn left and walk down to the bottom of the bank, climb over the stile beside a metal gate and walk under the M40. On the other side, cross another stile and walk ahead beside a wire fence. When the fence swings abruptly to the right, continue ahead to a stile. Cross this and the plank bridge beyond it and then veer right to pass through a metal kissing gate. Now swing slightly left and walk up the grassy incline, now alongside another wire fence on the other side of which, in Umberslade Park, tall Wellingtonia trees stand with their heads high, dwarf-

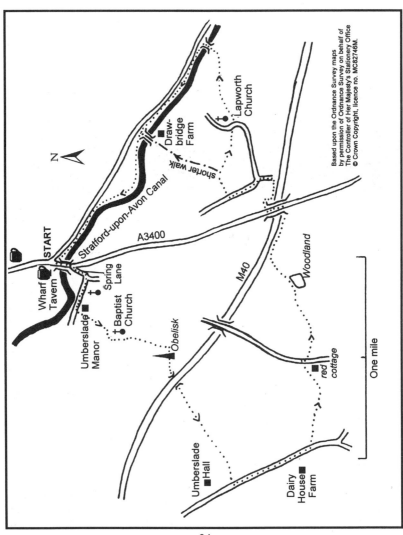

The mysterious obelisk, probably dating from 1747

ing their neighbours. Umberslade Hall soon comes into view ahead on your right.

Built in 1680, Umberslade Hall was the seat of the Archer family. During World War II, it housed Belgian and Czech troops, but it is now divided into luxury flats.

Continue through two more metal kissing gates beyond which the path becomes enclosed. Maybe sending a startled pheasant or two scurrying for cover as you go, continue on this path soon to reach a road onto which you turn left. Walk on, passing further fine trees on your left until, just over 100 yards after the timber-framed house and barn at Dairy House Farm, take a waymarked path to the left. This, in 15 yards, swings left and then right, soon to cross a field to the left of double wooden electricity posts.

As you near the far side of this field, Lapworth Church comes into view between farm buildings half-left ahead. After the stile, proceed with the wire fence on your right and then swing right to walk around the right edge of the fenced-off, wooded area which confronts you. Cross a stile by a pool and walk on, bearing slightly left and aiming for an electricity post 50 yards to the left of a steep-roofed, red cottage. The stile in the corner of this field soon leads to a lane into which you turn right. You reach the red cottage in 50 yards and cross the stile (on the left) nearly opposite to it.

Walk half-right across the field, soon crossing ridge and furrow, to cross a stile in its far right-hand corner. Now aim for the large patch of trees directly ahead across this field (*not* the smaller, more compact one slightly to your right). As you approach your target woodland, you will be able to see, towards its left side, the bare trunks of two Scots pine trees in front of which is your next stile. Having negotiated this, walk down towards the motorway, bearing slightly right, crossing a stile and a muddy bridge *en route*.

After the bridge, veer right and walk along the motorway boundary until, just after the first lamp standard on the slip road, cross a stile and walk up a short bank to the pavement. Cross the slip road to the opposite pavement and walk on a few yards until you are on the bridge with the motorway beneath you. When the traffic on this busy A3400 permits, cross to the other side of the bridge, turn left and walk on, northwards. At lamp standard no. 44, by the roundabout beyond the bridge, turn right onto a tarmacked path which, in 30 yards, turns abruptly to the right.

Follow this bridleway and at the motorway fencing, turn left and pass through a gate, continuing by the fencing across rough ground (by-passing an awkward bramble patch as you go!) until you reach another gate in front of spindly pine trees. Go through the gate, turn left and, leaving the noisy motorway behind you, walk up a mossy asphalt track to a lane (Church Lane) which became a cul-de-sac when the motorway was built. Continue along this lane and at the T-junction, bear left. After about 275 yards cross a stile on your right and walk down the field with the hedge on your left, Lapworth Church being prominent ahead. Just after the next stile, the two routes diverge.

For the **longer** *route continue reading from* ★ *below.*

Following the **shorter** route, now aim down the slope for the far right-hand corner of the field where you cross a stile beside a quiet brook and walk on crossing a stile beside a gateway on the far side of the field. Now walk straight up the incline to reach another stile-by-gateway. Cross this and walk ahead alongside a line of oaks after the sixth of which the path leads through the farmyard of Drawbridge Farm and soon reaches the Stratford-upon-Avon Canal. Cross the drawbridge and turn left onto the towpath, joining the longer route at ✪ on page 27.

★ Following the **longer** route, fork three-quarters right down the slope to a stout, sleeper bridge beyond which is a stile. Cross these and walk straight ahead across two fields to the church. Enter the churchyard by the gate on the right.

St Mary's Church, Lapworth is a fine old building, the pinnacled grey stone walls of which are picturesque in bright sunlight. The tower is almost detached from the church on the north side and, within the church, the Norman nave and other features, dating from the eleventh century to more modern times, provide great interest.

A scene from bygone times

After leaving the main door on the south side of the church, turn left and walk across the churchyard to pass through red brick gate posts beyond a line of old lime trees. A gravel path ends at a narrow lane which you cross and climb the stile on the other side. Walk ahead parallel to the boundary on your left to cross a stile in the facing hedge. The path now curves down to the right past newly-planted trees.

Just beyond a pool, the path swings right to a low stile which you cross. Continue up the incline, initially with another tree-fringed pool on your right, to cross a stile some 20 yards from the far, right-hand corner of the field. 150 yards ahead, you reach a stile but you do not pass over this, turning left just before it to walk beside the wooden palings round the edge of Lapworth Cricket Club. Passing through a wicket gate, turn right then left and cross canal bridge number 30. Reaching the towpath on the other side, turn left and, after just over half a mile, reach a drawbridge (28) where you may be joined by those who have taken the shorter route.

✪ Continue on the towpath, soon seeing ornamental domestic fowl, going under bridge 27 and past another drawbridge (26). Soon after passing under bridge 25, take a path up to the right which leads through the car park of the Wharf Tavern to your starting point.

Drawbridge on the Stratford Canal

6
Ancient and Modern – a Circuit from Kingswood Junction

This figure-of-eight walk starkly contrasts the tranquillity of canal travel with the more-modern methods which have superseded it, the motorways and railways.

Start: Kingswood Junction (GR186710)
Distance: 9 miles (with half mile diversion to Rowington); shorter option 6 miles (with half mile diversion to Rowington).
Maps: Landranger 139/151; Pathfinder 954, 975 & 976.
Parking: Car park and picnic area, Kingswood Junction
Public Transport: Some trains between Birmingham and Leamington Spa stop at Lapworth Station. If travelling by train, on leaving the station turn right into Station Lane and then turn right again at the T-junction at Old Warwick Road. Go under the railway and over the canal, then turn left to reach the car park and picnic area at Kingswood junction. (From the station to the start of the walk is about half a mile.)
Refreshments: Tom o' the Wood.

FROM the picnic area, walk to the Stratford-upon-Avon Canal and turn right along the towpath. Pass bridge 36 (on your left) but do not cross it, continuing on the towpath past the British Waterways Office (at which interesting pamphlets may be obtained) and round the edge of the large canal basin. Walk on until you cross the (un-numbered) bridge which lies just beyond lock 22. Having done this, turn right and continue, now using the towpath on the east side of the canal. Continue, passing under the noisy M40 and seeing, *en route,* two of the barrel-roofed lock-keepers' cottages – it is said that the builders used the same pattern for the roofs as for the canal bridges. Having passed lock 24, for most of the next mile or so the far bank is lined with a near-unbroken line of alder trees.

The wood from alders was once important for making clogs. The tree is able to live in waterlogged conditions, aided by bacteria in swellings on its roots which enable it to make direct use of nitrogen gas, an important element in protein manufacture. Alders are now threatened by a water-borne fungus that may be as damaging to them as Dutch Elm Disease is to elms. Fortunately this has not yet reached the trees here although some are having to be cut down, and other coppiced, because their roots are causing damage to the canal banks.

Just over 200 yards after passing the brick piers of a disused railway bridge, cross the stile just after lock 30 at bridge 40 at Lowsonford and turn left to walk along a lane. (You have now joined the Heart of England Way). This lane goes up an incline and then across the M40 and the adjoining railway track. Just beyond the bridge, pass through a gateway on the right (notice the Heart of England waymarks) and walk down a track which leads towards the railway and then veers left and runs parallel to it as it climbs towards a relay-station of a mobile phone company. Here, follow the track as it turns sharply to the left.

You have now turned your back on the M40, once described by Vivian Bird as "a thoroughly needless motorway". The fifty-nine mile long Oxford to Birmingham section cost £293 million to build. At its opening, on January 16 1991, the then Secretary of State for Transport (Malcolm Rifkind) admitted that "this road passes through some of England's finest countryside" and went on to say that "it is a tribute to the designers and engineers that the beauty of this country has been preserved".

Walk on with the hedge on your left, soon passing a thicket in which is a dilapidated footbridge made of railway sleepers. Notice also, in summer, the

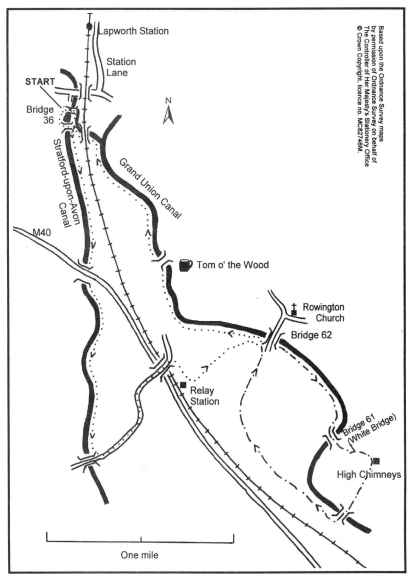

profuse, scrambling growth of goosegrass (or cleavers) in the hedgerow at your left hand.

Walking on, the path swings right as you pass along the top edge of a deep cutting on the Grand Union Canal, a feature referred to later. After two hundred yards or so, the path emerges from the field onto a lane adjacent to bridge 62 over the canal.

Here you have three options:

- To turn left and cross the bridge and walk up to Rowington village in order to visit the Church of St Laurence. (This is referred to, but not visited, on Walk 8 of *Country Walks*.) In common with many country churches, this is generally kept locked when services are not being held, the author, having paid several visits, never having been fortunate to find it open! This diversion would add about half a mile to the walk.

- Rejoin the route at ★ on page 31, having opted out of the southern loop of this walk.

- Continue on the southern loop as described below.

Cross the lane and pass through a gap by a redundant stile on the opposite side of the lane to reach a path leading down to the towpath. Carry on in the same direction until bridge 61 is reached. Go under this bridge (called White Bridge, presumably because of its white-painted, wooden balustrade) and, immediately on the other side, use steps to reach a rough track, noticing the 'Walkers Welcome' signs. Use this to cross the bridge and walk on, bearing left by a large, nearly-dead ash tree and farm buildings, up to a cluster of houses dominated by one called High Chimneys.

The two tall chimneys of his house make it conspicuous for miles around. You may ponder over the extensions, each complete with a door and a tiled roof, which are built onto the chimneys, high-up. Are these the ultimate in 'penthouse flats'?

Follow the track as it bears right in front of the buildings. 20 yards or so after the houses, as it divides and curves further right, follow it down to cross the canal at bridge 60 (marked on the OS map as Castle Meadow Bridge). Having crossed the bridge, follow the same heading until you reach a waymarked stile. Do not cross this, but turn right and walk with a wire-netting fence at your left hand. In about 250 yards, pass, but do not cross, another stile leading to a footbridge.

This woodland, on both sides of the canal, has been privately planted with grant-aid from the Forestry Commission and its owners welcome walkers. The 65 hectare area contains short-term trees like poplar but is predominantly planted with oak and ash and so will gradually re-establish the type of woodland which was to be seen many years ago before the Forest of Arden was cleared.

Keep to the periphery of the woodland as the character of the area will change drastically as the seedlings and saplings mature. This boundary is far from straight so, for the next mile, meander with the rabbit-proof fence, keeping it on your left-hand side and, maybe, noticing wooden badger gates, these hinged at the top and which can be pushed open by badgers (and, presumably, foxes) but not by rabbits.

Follow the fence's many changes of direction (some abrupt) until you reach the next stile (lower part wire-netted). (As you cross this, you will see red-brick farm buildings a quarter of a mile away on your right.) In 10 yards, reach a track. Turn right onto this and immediately pass through a waymarked gate and follow the bridleway ahead, which can be muddy at times. Going up the slope, the track goes to the left of metal farm gates and leads back to bridge 62 on the Grand Union Canal.

★ *Here, those who opted out of the southern loop re-join the main path.*

Just before its *left* hand parapet, negotiate a metal barrier and use a slanting path to reach the towpath.

As you walk through this 200 yard long cutting try to think back to when it was being excavated in the 1790s. There were no mechanical aids then. Pick-and-shovel-and-sweat were the main options available, with horses to haul the laden wheelbarrows up steep ramps to the top of the ever-deepening trench. The heavily-wooded banks are now draped with abundant wild clematis (Old Man's Beard, Father Christmas and Traveller's Joy are amongst its common names), the fluffy seed-heads of which can be spectacular in winter sunshine.

Continue along the towpath, maybe diverting at bridge 63 for rest and refreshment at Tom o' the Wood, a public house. Then walk on until you reach a canal T-junction. Do not cross the bridge but turn left (the signpost opposite directs you to Stratford) and walk about 150 yards along a short stretch of canal which leads back to Kingswood Junction.

This is the Lapworth Link. Opened in 1802 to link the Stratford-upon-Avon Canal with the Warwick and Birmingham Canal (as it was then called), it was abandoned and filled in a few years later after disagreements between the two canal companies. Reopened in the mid-1990s, the Link provides (literally) a short cut between the two canals, by-passing locks 20 and 21 and thus saving two lockfuls of water (about 50,000 gallons) per boat passage.

At the top of the Link, cross the recently-built, brick bridge just to the right of Canal Cottage, another barrel-roofed house. Then, pass lock 20 and the house near it which, apparently, stands on one of Britain's smallest islands! Having crossed bridge 36, turn right to reach your starting point and complete your figure-of-eight.

7

More Meanderings Around Alvechurch and Rowney Green

Two pleasant, undulating routes which explore the complicated footpath network connecting these two places.

> **Start:** The Square, in the centre of Alvechurch village.(GR029726)
> **Distance:** 7½ miles; shorter option 4 miles.
> **Maps:** Landranger 139; Pathfinder 954.
> **Parking:** There is a free car park off Tanyard Lane which branches off Red Lion Street by the Red Lion public house just north of The Square in Alvechurch. To get to The Square from the car park, take either of the paths at the sides of the Methodist Church.
> **Public Transport:** Midland Red bus service number 146 connecting Birmingham and Evesham serves Alvechurch.
> Trains on the Cross-City Rail line from Lichfield to Redditch stop at Alvechurch station. Turn right when leaving the platform and start your walk from ★ below.
> **Refreshments:** The Red Lion and The Swan, both in Alvechurch.

FROM The Square walk up Bear Hill and, after about 50 yards, branch up a tarmacked drive on the left which ends in the churchyard of St Laurence's church. Walk ahead, passing the church on your right hand side and, just beyond it, an ancient, hollow-trunked yew held together by metal tie-bars.

○ *Railway travellers, nearing the end of their walk, rejoin the route here.*

Leave the churchyard via metal gates and walk on down a lane soon to reach Station Road (which is the continuation of Bear Hill). Veer left into Station Road and, in about 100 yards, take a footpath to the left which leads, behind houses, to Alvechurch Station. Turn left into the station approach.

★ *If you have travelled by train join the walk here.*

Walk on, with the railway track on your right side, passing in front of the former station buildings which have now been converted for office use. After crossing a stile, continue with the railway on your right to reach a footbridge and stile which you cross. These are maintained by the Alvechurch Village Society, members of which do much good on behalf of walkers in this area. Walk half left up the incline and, at the field's brow, look for a prominent clump of holly trees in the hedge below. Aim for the stile a little to the left of these trees. (Some writers believe that holly trees were left to grow tall in hedges as stile markers.)

Having crossed the stile, turn left and walk on with the hedge on your left. At the end of the field, cross a stile and bear slightly left to cross another one. Now go two thirds left to reach a rather inconspicuous stile in paddock railings. Cross this, walk forward across a metalled drive and then across the end of a recently-planted spinney, the cherry trees in which make a pretty display in spring. Cross the stile ahead and then aim for the far left-hand corner of the field where a stile (which is in front of a converted barn) gives you access to a road (Grange Lane). Here turn left and continue along Grange Lane soon to cross the River Arrow and to reach the busy Redditch Road. Cross this with care, turn left and then take the first turn on the right (The

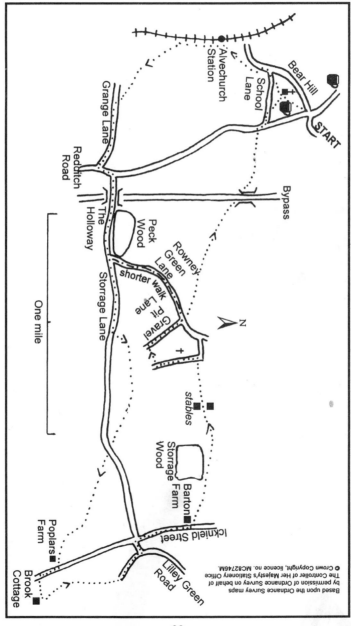

© Crown Copyright, licence no. MC82746M.
The Controller of Her Majesty's Stationery Office
by permission of Ordnance Survey on behalf of
Based upon the Ordnance Survey maps

Holloway). Proceed up the slope and, about 350 yards after crossing over the Alvechurch bypass, reach Rowney Green Lane.

Since passing over the bypass, you have been walking past Peck Wood on your left, the entrance to the wood being a short distance down Rowney Green Lane. Peck Wood, owned by local circuits of the Methodist Church, is private woodland which is carpeted with bluebells in their flowering season. On specific dates in late April and early May, the woodland is open to the public, details of these dates being available by telephoning 01527 61396.

If you are using the **shorter** option, turn left into Rowney Green Lane and walk on it towards the village of Rowney Green and, opposite Gravel Pit Lane, turn left towards Newbourne Wood Nature Reserve, rejoining the main route at ✿ on page 35.

Following the **longer** route walk straight ahead up Storrage Lane. (This has no pavement and, particularly when the road narrows after a short distance, it is advisable to walk on the right-hand side, preferably in single file.) There are good views to the right over the Worcestershire countryside to the south. After an initial gentle climb, the road descends and, just after a patch of woodland on the left, cross a stile on the left (under a holly tree!). Walk on, with the woodland close at your left hand, to cross a ditch via a hurdle-stile and rough bridge (under yet another holly tree!).

Having done this, continue down the slope veering slightly to the right towards a waymarked stile in front of a red-brick house. Do *not* cross this stile but turn right to follow the hedge which separates you from a stream. Continue alongside the hedge and stream through two long fields which may be divided by ropes and electric fences (easily negotiated!) into several horse paddocks.

After passing (and ignoring) two further waymarked stiles on the left, the second field gradually becomes narrower and, about 70 yards before its end, you finally cross the stream by a footbridge on your left. On the other side of the bridge, turn three-quarters right to walk towards a pair of stiles by which you cross Storrage Lane. On the other side, follow a rough cart track and cross a stile on the left-hand side of a farm gate. Going slightly to the left of your previous heading, you reach a concrete bridge which connects you to the next field.

Go ahead, passing just to the right of a fenced-off area (in which are a couple of large trees) and then to the left of an isolated oak, 100 yards beyond which you walk to the left of a pool. Now bear half-right to a prominent stile. Cross this, pass through a small spinney and then use another stile plus two plank bridges to reach a field. Walk on with the hedge near your left side. Immediately after a substantial, metal farm gate, the hedge turns abruptly to the left for about twenty yards and then to the right.

About 50 yards further on, look for a stile on your left. This is hiding beneath a willow tree and is easily missed. Cross it and a footbridge and, reaching the next field, go half-left (walking past Poplars Farm on your right) aiming for a stile in front of the appropriately-named White House. Reaching the road, turn right and walk along the road for about about 75 yards and then turn left into the wide track signed Brook Cottage and leading to Brook Farm.

Walk on with the farm buildings on your right and, some twenty yards beyond the modern-built farmhouse, cross a wooden footbridge on the left over a dried-up stream. Go half left (NW) across the field to a waymarked footbridge which is about 15 yards to the left of a prominent ash tree. Keeping the boundary to your left, walk ahead for about 600 yards, crossing a farm track and a stile *en route*. Just before a house, cross a stream by means of a footbridge on your left, and then go two-thirds right to squeeze through a metal kissing gate.

The following definition of a kissing gate was included in a description of a Cotswold ramble in the May 25 1997 edition of the New York Times: 'A sideways arch is hung from a fence post, with a hinged gate swung from the post opposite. Push the gate open, press your body against the top of the arch, swing the gate and exit. The name derives from the supposed habit of country boys trapping girls inside and saying "Give me a kiss and I'll let you through"'.

Having negotiated this, turn left and walk along a rough lane towards a busy road (Lilley Green Road). Turn left and use its wide grass verge to walk a short distance to a road junction. Turn right, briefly re-acquainting yourself with Storrage Lane, in 30 yards turning right into Icknield Street. Walk along this old Roman road until, just beyond the first farm (Barton Farm), cross a stile on your left leading to an enclosed path which soon delivers you into a field. Walk up the incline with Storrage Wood on your left.

When you reach the brow of the hill, Rowney Green village coming into view directly ahead, pass through a gateway. Ignoring a rough path ahead, aim slightly right to encounter a waymarked oak tree. Continue on this heading, pass through a cross-hedge and walk down the slope with a much-neglected hedge on your right. At the bottom of the field, cross a wooden footbridge, turn left and follow the hedge for about 50 yards to reach a stile on the left. Cross this, bear left for 10 yards, then right to cross another stream. Having done this, walk across the field to a stile opposite and then use its waymark to indicate your line up the field to cross stiles between stables.

Continue up a rough lane. When its surface suddenly improves, turn left into Chapel Lane, soon passing the tiny Rowney Green Shared Church (to which reference was made on Walk 9 in *Country Walks*). Proceed down the lane, again with good views of Worcestershire ahead. In about 250 yards, you reach a patch of woodland. At the bottom end of this, take a right turn and join a path which wanders with the southern boundary of the woodland. When the path finally reaches a lane (Gravel Pit Lane), turn right and walk up the lane to its junction with Rowney Green Lane. Go straight ahead onto a path to Newbourne Wood Nature Reserve.

✿ *Here the two routes join.*

Walk straight ahead until, at the end of a horse paddock, your path swings left and continues between tall Scots pines. The path soon slopes down, the descent being assisted by a flight of concrete steps. Skirting to the left of a thicket 30 yards ahead, take a clear path down the hill aiming for Alvechurch church, with good views of the Lickey Hills beyond. Continue onward in roughly the same direction, going down the slope and then up an incline beyond passing two stiles, a footbridge and a kissing gate *en route*.

The path then veers slightly to the right, over the field brow to a stile leading to a lane. Cross the stile, turn left into the lane and follow it under the bypass, over the Arrow and back to the Redditch Road. Turn right and immediately left into School Lane. Walk up the lane for about 100 yards, taking a right turn to walk on a footpath opposite St Mary's RC Church and soon pass through a kissing gate into the churchyard of St Lawrence Church.

If you have travelled by train turn left and walk past the church and then follow the instructions from ❸ *at the beginning of the walk.*

If you started at The Square turn right by the church and walk down the lane to Bear Hill and your starting point.

8
Bromsgrove and some Housman Connections

An undulating walk which contrasts the bustle of a market town, the sound and fury of a motorway and the peace and quiet of delightful countryside and charming woodlands.

> **Start:** The A.E.Housman statue in the pedestrianised High Street in Bromsgrove, just under 150 yards from its junction with Stratford Road. (GR958706)
> **Distance:** 8 miles.
> **Maps:** Landranger 139; Pathfinder 953.
> **Parking:** Public car parks in Bromsgrove.
> **Public Transport:** Midland Red West services 142,143 & 144 (If arriving from the Birmingham direction on a 142 or 143 service you can shorten the walk and avoid some road walking if you alight in Bromsgrove at the junction of Broad Street and Crabtree Lane. Then start reading from the third paragraph below.)
> **Refreshments:** The New Inn, Bournheath and numerous facilities in Bromsgrove.

The statue of Alfred Edward Housman, by Kenneth Potts, was unveiled in 1985. Born in 1859 (you will see his birthplace later), Housman was educated at Bromsgrove School and at St John's College, Oxford. A scholar and poet, perhaps his best-known work being 'A Shropshire Lad'.

CLOSE to the statue, walk down Mill Lane and cross Market Street. On the other side, turn left and walk past a supermarket and then turn right in Church Street. Stay on this road (which becomes Crabtree Lane), walking beside a large cemetery.

When you come to Church Road continue ahead along Crabtree Lane and stay on it for about a quarter of a mile and, when it begins to get narrower, turn left into Parkwood Road and, in 20 yards, go right into Lynden Close. Walk to the end of this quiet cul-de-sac where you pass through a metal kissing gate after which you veer left for a few yards and then walk ahead, with a tall hedge at your left hand, through this market-gardening area.

When you emerge onto a road, opposite you, a little to the right, you will see a very unpromising, padlocked gate beside which is a tall, metal kissing gate. Squeeze through this and walk ahead on a lane, soon to reach a path overshadowed by tall cupressus trees, with orchards on either side. Cross the M5 motorway by way of a footbridge, go down steps on the other side, cross a stile and soon drop down to a wooden footbridge. Having crossed this, go ahead on a well-used path through two fields, the second much larger than the first.

Passing Fockbury Farm you may get distant views of the Malverns to the left before reaching a lane. Cross the lane and the stile opposite and follow the clear path which goes up the field straight ahead of you. Aim just to the right of a row of holly bushes at the top of the slope where you clamber over a rough stile . Continue half-left from your former heading, Dodford church soon coming into view ahead on your left.

After crossing two more stiles, your path drops steeply through a strip of woodland at the bottom of which you cross a stream by way of a footbridge and then turn left. Cross another stile and walk through a paddock which you leave by way of a stile on your right, just before a yew tree of near-perfect symmetry protected by iron railings. Turn left onto a concrete-surfaced bridleway which leads down to a road.

Bear slightly right as you cross the road to climb over a stile which leads to an enclosed path. This ultimately gives way to a lane which you follow until it turns off to the right. Here you go straight ahead across a stile and walk on down an incline towards woodland. Your next objective soon comes into view – a footbridge. Having gone over this, bear right to climb a stile and enter High Wood.

This wood is bedecked in early spring with white flowers slightly tinged with purple. These are wood anemones and Richard Mabey, in his Flora Britannica, recounts what is perhaps the most charming of child mispronunciations of any name – wooden enemies.

Continue on the path straight ahead as it climbs gently for a little over 100 yards when you reach a path-junction. Here join the path going down to the right and stay on it for about 600 yards as it wanders through the wood and approaches a red-brick house, High Wood Cottage.

Just beyond this, turn right onto a bridleway soon passing through two wooden wicket gates as you initially walk along the edge of Big Wood. A third wicket gate admits you into the wood where you continue ahead on a sometimes-muddy track until a final wicket gate gives access to a road.

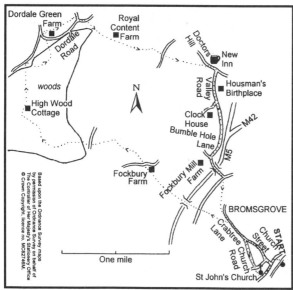

Here, turn right and, in less that 10 yards, climb a stile on your right, cross the paddock ahead and pass over another stile which leads into Nutnells Wood. A clear path leads you through the wood which you soon leave by crossing a stile at the other side. Continue along the wood's edge until, having crossed the next stile, you negotiate another on your immediate left which leads you back into the wood. Soon cross two plank bridges and then take the right fork onto another clear path which leads you through the wood until you emerge into a paddock across which you bear left and walk to a stile at its far side.

Reaching Dordale Road, turn left and, immediately beyond Dordale Green Farm, turn right onto a signposted path. Soon after passing through two metal farm gates, with an ornamental pool to your right, go slightly right up a gentle incline to a stile at the top. Continue ahead, on roughly the same heading, for about 300 yards, through two fields, to go over a stile leading to a lane. Here turn right and, in less than 100 yards turn left to join Dordale Road again.

In just over 100 yards, cross a stile on your right, pass a barn, go over a hurdle stile and walk on, with a wire fence on your right, to cross another stile. Having done this, continue on the same

The Housman statue in Bromsgrove High Street

heading across the next field to a stile at the other side. Cross this and, with a hedge still at your left hand, walk on a gentle slope up the next field, noticing as you go the newly-rebuilt Royal Content Farm mentioned on Walk 15 in *Country Walks*.

At the top, cross the stile ahead of you and continue, now hugging the hedge on your right first passing through a paddock that you leave by a stile. After the next stile (an awkward one where an old tree stump may help you to cross a rather boggy area), veer slightly left up the slope to reach and cross another stile. Having done this, walk ahead on your former heading across the undulating meadow.

Cross a stile beneath an oak tree, turn left and walk for 20 yards to climb over another stile. Immediately turn right and proceed straight ahead, with the hedge on your right, until, having negotiated two more stiles, you reach a road. Cross this and the stile opposite and walk on, soon to descend a grassy slope at the bottom of which, near dilapidated ash trees, you climb over another stile.

Go up the next slope, with its boundary on your left, and at the field's end, by a pool, do *not* go through the wicket gate on your left but proceed to the right of the pool where you cross a stile. Walk down another grassy bank and, following the line of an overhead cable, continue by a hedge on your left until you come to another stile. Go over this and follow the hedge as it veers to the left, soon to reach a stile which leads you, via a short drive, onto a road (Doctor's Hill). Here, turn right and walk down the road, passing the New Inn, and shortly turn right into Valley Road.

In a couple of hundred yards, from the security of a short pavement, you will see, on the third house, a blue plaque.

This is the walk's second contact with Housman and the plaque informs you that he was born here on 26 March 1859. He and his family moved away whilst he was still an infant. They later lived at Fockbury House, later known as The Clock House, and it was there that the poet spent his youth between 1873 and 1878. You will see what remains of this house shortly.

Continue along Valley Road and when, in about 200 yards, it swings off to the right, go with it but note the delightfully-named cul-de-sac, Bumble Hole Lane, on your left. 100 yards further on you come to the site of the seventeenth century Fockbury House (referred to above) with another blue plaque, all that remains of it being the ivy-covered clock tower. Having seen this, walk back to the way you have come and turn right to walk down Bumble Hole Lane. On your way, you pass Bumble Hole Cottage which incorporates an old church building and sports a notice saying:

> NO BEGGING
> OR
> PLEADING
> By The Gracious Ordinance Of The Honourable Lords
> Of The Royal Courts Of Justice
> LONDON ENGLAND
> Dated 1871

The surface of the lane then deteriorates and you soon become very aware of the junction between the M5 and the M42, St John's Church, Bromsgrove being visible ahead beneath one of the flyovers. At a path junction just before the flyover, take the right hand option and continue on the rough track, soon with the carriageway high above you. On emerging onto a road, turn left.

Passing Fockbury Mill Farm and several barn conversions, soon cross the motorway – all nine, busy lanes of it! As the motorway noise quickly recedes, walk on to turn right into Perryfields Road and, when the traffic allows, cross it and immediately bear left down a rough lane which soon becomes a farm track. After about 80 yards, bear left at a path junction and notice, on the horizon straight ahead of you, the slender spire of Tardebigge church.

The track soon veers right and, when you reach houses, continue on a road and walk ahead onto Crabtree Lane. When this widens, you will be covering ground walked earlier in the day. Stay on Crabtree Lane until, opposite Coronation Cottage (now a shop and built in 1911 around the time of the crowning of King George V), turn right into Church Road. Pass New

Road and when you come to a junction, cross Church Lane and enter the graveyard of St John's Church, Bromsgrove.

As you bear left across the burial ground, which contains gravestones dating as far back as 1567, notice, prominent on the church's north side, a pair of black-and-white memorials which commemorate the deaths of Thomas Scaife and Joseph Rutherford who lost their lives when the boiler of their railway engine exploded in November 1840. The stones bear verses, one of which starts thus: 'My engine now is cold and still, no water does my boiler fill'.

Leave the churchyard at its south-east end via the Forty Eight Steps (in fact, only 42), seeing (hopefully, not too late!) notices at the top and bottom which say 'Please beware – uneven steps'. Turning left and crossing the road, you soon return to your starting place.

One of the railwaymen's graves in Bromsgrove churchyard

41

9
Beoley and Hob Hill

Start: War Memorial near Beoley church on Church Hill (GR065696).
Distance: 4½ miles; shorter option 1½ miles.
Maps: Landranger 139; Pathfinder 954/975.
Parking: Near Beoley church.
Public Transport: Midland Red service 178 (Birmingham/Redditch) stops at Beoley Church.
Refreshments: The Village Inn, Holt End.

In the field on the opposite side of Church Hill to the war memorial is an ancient earthwork which may have marked the activities of neolithic man some 3000 years ago.

WALKING from the memorial, notice the giant sycamore tree near the top, left hand corner of the car park, but leave the car park via a wicket gate at its top right hand corner. Walk ahead and soon swing right to join a path, enclosed by wooden railings, which soon slopes down, becoming fringed with tall poplar trees. At the end of the path, cross a stile and walk on following the hedge on the right as it curves to the right.

After about 100 yards the hedge swings sharp right and you will see the remains of an old, metal cattle trough under an oak. Here turn left and walk across the grassland as it begins to slope down towards a stile to the right of a small wood. Cross this stile and continue ahead, initially past a pool, with the fence at your left hand. At the field's end cross a stile on the left.

Here the two routes diverge. For the **longer** *route continue from ★ below.*

Following the **shorter** option, continue straight ahead after crossing the stile, walking in the direction of Rowney Green village on the distant hill. Pass through a gate and walk on a track which curves to the left beside a pool. Just beyond the pool, pass through another gate and turn right to walk on a track beside a football pitch. Beyond the pitch, near a dilapidated henhouse, turn left and walk ahead to the footbridge over which those using the longer route would have come. Do not cross the bridge, but now follow the text from ✪ on page 45.

★ To follow the **longer** route, turn right after crossing the stile and continue, on your former heading, now with the hedge on your right. Cross another stile and, about 100 yards beyond this, the hedge angles off to the right. At this point, you go half left across the field to a stile at the bottom of the gentle incline. Cross this stile and, keeping on more-or-less the same heading, cross a sleeper bridge and then a further stile. Your path now gently slopes up across the field, gradually getting closer to the right-hand field boundary. When you meet this boundary, you will see a stile beneath two oaks, one large and one smaller. Cross this stile and walk between twin pools to another stile. Climb over this and, accompanied by a fence and hedge for the first 80 yards or so, walk straight ahead to climb over a further stile. Now walk up the slope, passing between small pools and a Christmas tree plantation.

Cross a stile and go through a small field. Cross another stile and go straight ahead, passing a vehicle and caravan park. Cross a farm track (more caravans to the left) and go up a grassy slope and through the farmyard of Chapel Farm to reach a road (Carpenters Hill). Immediately, turn left onto a track which can be extremely muddy after wet weather but whose high verges may provide a drier passage. Continue along this track for nearly half a mile. Just before you reach a large patch of holly bushes, turn to follow another track that veers off to the right, the main track swinging left. (You will rejoin the track here, later.)

The holly is our commonest evergreen tree. Only the female plants bear berries,

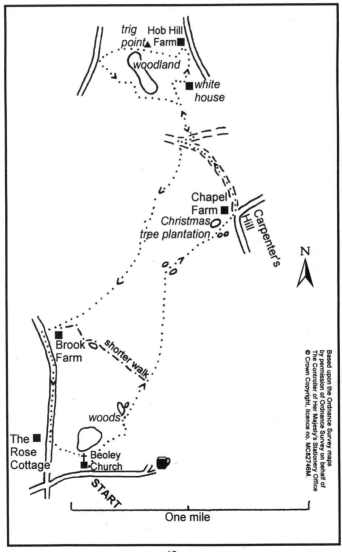

so the females in this area seem to be outnumbered by the males.

About 20 yards after joining the new track, cross a stile on the left which is overhung with more holly. Walk onwards with the field boundary on your left, soon crossing a sandy horse-gallop. *Watch out for approaching horses.* At the end of the field, pass through a gate (to which you will return after the Hob Hill loop).

On this loop you may feel that the route is very angular and shortcuts might attract you. However, the route follows the rights-of-way and we must adhere to these!

Continue on the same heading, now with the fence on the right. At this field's end, pass through a farm gate on your right and walk down a rough lane for about 80 yards. Just before a white house, turn left past lichen-encrusted staddle stones and cross a stile. Walk onwards with the hedge on your right until, after about 150 yards, you pass through a row of well-spaced oak trees.

Having done this, veer slightly left (aiming for right-hand end of wooden palings) to reach a stile into a lane. Do not cross this stile – turn your back on it and walk away from it now with the wooden palings of Hob Hill Farm on your right-hand side. As you go, you may check the time on a clock over a garage block topped with a racehorse weather vane and admire horses' faces as they stare at you from their stables.

At the corner of the fence, squeeze between it and a hedge and go half right onto very rough ground. After passing mounds of stable waste, veer further right aiming for a stile which is five yards to the left of an oak tree the trunk of which is heavily swollen with burrs which make it, at a distance, look like a large Brussels sprout plant. 100 yards beyond the stile is a triangulation point marking Hob Hill's modest summit of just less than 600 feet.

There are about 6000 trig pillars (that's the official name) in the UK. Only about 2000 of these are still used by the Ordnance Survey, their role being replaced by the Global Positioning System using satellites. Some of the redundant pillars have been 'adopted' and are looked after by members of the public - this one has already been fostered.

Pass the trig point and walk on in the same direction. As you reach trees which ring the top of the hill's western and southern slopes, the path begins to descend and swing to the left. Walking down to a stile just right of a red-brick house at the foot of the slope, you may contemplate the impact that the M42 has made on the tranquillity of this area. When you reach the stile, do not cross onto the road beyond but face away from it and walk one-third right (S.E.) round the shoulder of the hill aiming just to the right of the tree ring.

On reaching the trees, continue to circle left round the shoulder of the hill, aiming for a gateway beside one of the largest of the oaks which are interspersed in the boundary fence ahead of you. Straight ahead of you is another large stand of trees and your next objective is a stile which lies just to the right of these, again in the shade of an oak.

Cross this stile and continue up the incline shadowing the woodland fence as it curves to the left. Climb over a stile beside a gate and then proceed, half-right, up the slope to reach the gate in the right-hand corner of the field through which you passed to start the loop. Go through this gate and retrace your steps across the field (boundary now on your right) to reach the stile . Cross this, turn right onto the track and, soon passing the holly patch at your left hand, continue for about 50 yards until you see a stile on your left beside a metal gate and close behind an ivy-clad oak. Go over this and, as you stand with your back to it, half-right you will see the tops of a patch of trees.

Walk towards the left end of this woodland and you will pass round a redundant stile, walk down a slope past tall gorse bushes and enter the woodland by another stile. Follow the path down, veer with it to the right and soon leave the wood via another stile. Beyond this, go half-left between gorse bushes and, passing an elbow in the hedge, go to a stile in the field's far corner. Having crossed this stile and negotiated the ditch beyond it, turn right and continue for a few yards to a stream.

Here, turn left and follow the stream down the field, crossing it but staying with it after it has made a sharp left-right twist. You then cross a hidden stile some 20 yards before the bottom corner of the field. Here turn left and walk down a gradual slope with the hedge and stream on your left. Continue for about half a mile passing an attractive pool on your left and negotiating, *en route*, first a very awkward, ramshackle stile, then a stile over barbed wire (a contradiction, indeed!) and finally, just beyond a clump of willows and just before an abandoned hen house, a sleeper bridge and stout, wooden stile. Just over 100 yards beyond the hen house, cross the stream by a footbridge and turn right. (You may have traversed this in the other direction on Walk 7).

○ *Here the shorter route joins the main route.*

Walk ahead past Brook Farm and Brook Cottage to the road. Turn left onto this busy road and walk ahead with caution, preferably on the right in single file. You soon pass a road sign warning motorists to beware of wildfowl – which may have strayed from nearby ornamental pools. Continue on the road for about 500 yards and, when you reach The Rose Cottage, cross a stile opposite it (on your left). Now go half-right up the slope towards the church which is at the highest point on the hill and is hidden by trees in the summer, crossing ridge-and-furrow as you go. To the left of the church, pass through an old metal kissing gate by the woodside and enter the churchyard, by a similar gate, on its north side.

The impressive church of St Leonard, Beoley with its origins in the twelfth century is, in common with other country churches these days, normally kept locked to protect it from thieves and vandals. The snowdrops in its churchyard are spectacular in early spring. Near its west end, you will see a white marble headstone bearing the following inscription: 'In grateful memory of James Davies, member of the Worcestershire Constabulary, who was murdered while in the execution of his duty near Weatheroak Hill in the early morning of 28th February 1885 aged 33 years leaving an example of faithful service to his native country'. The spot where Moses Shrimpton murdered P.C. Davies, about three miles up Ryknild Street, near the entrance to Alcott Farm, is marked by a simple stone inscribed 'J.D.1885'.

For refreshment the Village Inn is about three-quarters of a mile along Church Hill to the east. Public transport users can catch their bus there.

10
Gorcott Hill and Ullenhall

Pretty footpaths and quiet country lanes make this a pleasant circuit.

Start: Gorcott Hill road, (GR092687)
Distance: 7 miles.
Maps: Landranger 139/150; Pathfinder 975.
Parking: Roadside on the left at the start of the old Gorcott Hill road, now a cul-de-sac.
Public Transport: Trains on the Birmingham/Stratford-upon-Avon line stop at Danzey station (*request stop*). (*See box below for details of how to join the main walk.*)
Refreshments: The Hollybush Inn on Gorcott Hill (near the start) and the Winged Spur at Ullenhall.

WALK on along Gorcott Hill to reach a gravelly lay-by opposite the first house (and do read the dire warning on its gate!). On the north side of this lay-by, alongside a gate marked 'The Long Meadow', is a waymarked stile. Cross this and walk along an enclosed and somewhat overgrown pathway alongside a lorry park and stables. This leads to an open field (presumably the Long Meadow) and you walk ahead with, on your right side, Grove Wood at the far end of which the russet-coloured trunks of Scots pines can be appreciated in sunny weather. At the end of the field, a stile leads you to the busy Ullenhall Lane into which you turn right.

❇ *Rail travellers continue here.*

With caution, walk ahead on the right hand side of the road, soon passing a terrace of white-painted houses. After about 150 yards, the grass verge widens and achieves almost lawn-like quality. Continue and soon cross the end of the drive to The Dell House. A few yards from the start of the drive climb a waymarked post stile alongside a gate on the left. Walk through a

---

Rail Travellers

! *Joining up with the main route involves a walk along a lane that can be extremely muddy in wet periods.*

On leaving the platforms, walk up the station drive to the roadway onto which you turn left. Since there is no pavement, it is recommended that you cross the road as soon as possible and walk ahead on the right-hand side. 50 yards after the road crosses the railway, turn right and proceed on a farm lane over another railway bridge. This is the muddy lane! When, after about 150 yards, you reach a trio of gateways, chose the left hand option, walk down a slight incline at the bottom of which you cross a stream by way of a footbridge. Here, turn right and join the main route at ★ on page 49.

Then, on your return cross the stile and footbridge, go up the lane, crossing the railway and turning left along the road back to the railway station.

spinney and paddock to enter a field and then continue, with the hedge at your left, as you go down a gentle incline.

Walk on, more-or-less on the same heading and with the hedge still on your left, for the best part of a mile when you *ignore* a waymark which invites you to turn sharply to your left. Soon after this waymark, cross a stile between the hedge and a deep, tree-surrounded pit. Proceed, still hugging the hedge at your left hand until, 150 yards after the next stile, you are confronted with two options – ignore the often-muddy track which swings off to the left and pass through a gateway on the right which has concrete gateposts.

Walk onwards, soon passing between the hedge and some disused farm buildings. 150 yards beyond these buildings, the path becomes enclosed and crosses a wooden footbridge. Beyond this, bear half left and walk in a gentle arc round the edge of the grounds of a white house to cross its drive by way

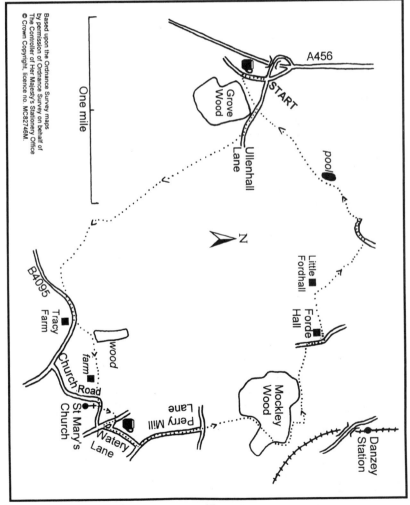

of a pair of waymarked stiles. Now bear very slightly right to a stile which leads to the B4095 Redditch to Henley-in-Arden road.

Turn left and, using the grass verge of this busy thoroughfare, walk on for 150 yards where, opposite Tracy Farm, you cross a stile. Walk ahead through newly-planted woodland, with the wire fence at your left side, until you reach a metal, farm gate. Here turn right, cross a stream via a plank bridge and negotiate a double stile. On the other side, bear slightly right to the edge of the mature woodland ahead. Walk on alongside this woodland (called The Reins) and, just beyond it, cross a stile on your left, turn right and continue on your former heading with the hedge now on your right.

At the field's end, cross another stile and walk on past a farm and then, just beyond a deep pit (or dried-up pool) on the right, cross a stile and (ignoring a misleading waymark) walk on, half left, towards a patch of trees to the right of red-brick houses. By way of a short, left/right zigzag involving two stiles, reach a road (Church Road). Cross the road to reach the church.

The yellow-stoned church of St Mary the Virgin, Ullenhall was built in 1875. It stands in a gravestone-free churchyard with, at its west end, a semicircle of four great Wellingtonia trees and, low down on the stone work, both grey and yellow lichens which thrive in this relatively unpolluted atmosphere.

Leaving the churchyard through its metal gates, cross the road again, go

through a metal kissing gate and walk across a field on a clear path to a similar gate and short, enclosed path which leads you to a road. You may choose to cross to a hostelry opposite.

The Winged Spur is the latest name for this public house which has, over the years, been called The Chathlow Arms, The Spur and Wing Inn and The Spur Inn. The coat-of-arms of the Knight family (mentioned as having many family members buried at the Old Chapel visited on Walk 12) included winged spurs, hence the current name.

To continue the walk, as you leave the pub, turn left and walk on down the road leaving the war memorial on your left. In about 100 yards, turn left into Watery Lane, soon to pass a display of old agricultural implements. Proceed along this lane, passing lions

To be used with a flying horse?

rampant on gateposts on your right and white-painted railings on your left. At a T-junction, turn left into Perry Mill Lane.

In about half a mile, you may notice, on the wall of the house at Elm Tree Farm, an old insurance token signifying cover by 'Farmers Fire and Life'. Just beyond this, you come to another T-junction. Here, cross the lane to climb over the stile opposite and, having done this, walk on to another waymarked stile to the left of a barn. Cross this and walk on keeping the tall, overgrown hedge (with, in late summer and autumn, its red hips and haws and its purple sloes) close at your right-hand side. Beyond the next stile, walk up a slight incline between tall, wire fences behind which deer were farmed. At the brow of the hill, you may wish to make use of a rustic-wood seat (Hadleigh's Walk) to enjoy the fine, long-distance views to the south and south east.

The question 'Who was Hadleigh?' has proved difficult to answer! However, after much research, it is established that Hadleigh was the name of a much-loved bassett hound who died on New Years' Eve and whose owners were Mr and Mrs Slater who live at Mockley Wood Farm. R.I.P. Hadleigh!

Hadleigh

Photograph by David Paton

Proceed onwards, keeping all the wooden palings on your left, soon to reach a comfortably designed stile leading to a bridleway. Beyond this, continue down an incline, initially through, but later, alongside, Mockley Wood. Soon after the railway line comes into view, the path swings left and, just after the second pool, you cross a stile and walk straight ahead across the field. At the other side, you come to a small complex of three gates, a stile and a footbridge which, unless you are going to return to Danzey station, you ignore and turn left.

★ *If you have come by train, join the walk and, later, leave it here. (See box on p. 46)*

Walk on with a stream (behind a hedge) on your right-hand side. You reach a stile and plank bridge which you cross and then bear left to follow an indistinct path through an overgrown area, passing the long-abandoned remains of a lorry still sporting painted-but-faded Union Jacks on its bonnet. Walk on with Mockley Wood on your left until, at the wood's end, you reach a stile. Cross this and the plank bridge beyond it, turn right and, following the line of the boundary, walk onwards to reach a lane.

Turn right into this and continue for a little over 150 yards until, just beyond a disused, red-brick barn (with its clock permanently showing the time as 4:10) in front of Forde Hall, turn left onto the concrete drive of the farm. Walk through the farmyard and, having passed the farmhouse at your left, soon veer right then left between farm buildings. Beyond the farmyard, walk ahead with electricity posts and wire fencing on your right. After the next stile, walk on to reach a waymark post at the boundary of the large grounds of Little Fordhall (an 'e' seems to have gone missing over the years!). Turn right here, cross a slatted bridge and, just beyond the next stile, turn left and (in 20 yards or so) right on to a tarmacked drive.

Continue up the slight incline, passing a pool and, then, a cattle grid beyond which the surface becomes rougher and the incline a little steeper. Tanworth-in-Arden church soon comes into view to the right. At the end of this drive, cross another cattle grid, turn left into a lane and, in a very few yards, take the right hand drive leading towards The Grange.

Follow this concrete-surfaced drive for about 75 yards and then swing right, a (blue) bridleway mark directing you towards Oakwood Farm and Grange Farm. Just beyond barns, follow the *blue* markers through a gate until, just before a derelict cottage, you cross a yellow waymarked stile on the left, followed very shortly by another one. Bear half right across the next field until, near its bottom right-hand corner, you cross a stile under a large oak tree. Bear right and continue up the incline with the boundary on your right.

At the field's end, cross a stile which is 10 yards or so to the left of a farm gate. Bear a quarter left and, as you come over the brow of the hill, you will see a stile at the bottom. Walk down to this, passing a large pool on your right. Beyond the stile, go half right for 35 yards to reach another stile beside a hollow oak (having crossed a sleeper bridge *en route*). Cross this stile, go straight ahead with, for the first 50 yards or so, the hedge on your right. The hedge then branches off the right and the path goes across the field (W) and, after the second of two stiles, turns left to cross a wooden footbridge. Beyond this, turn right and aim for a stile some 30 yards to the right of the terrace of white-painted cottages in front of which you passed earlier (if you started from Gorcott Hill).

In late September, you may see in this field some giant white puffballs, some exceeding two feet in diameter and containing unimaginably-large numbers of spores. Said by some to be edible – they are best left alone unless you know which species you are dealing with.

If you travelled by train, after crossing the stile out of the 'puffball' field, turn left and walk along Ullenhall Lane as at ❂ near the beginning of the text.

Having crossed the stile, carefully cross the road to another stile which leads to Long Meadow through which you retrace your steps to your starting place.

11
Hatton Locks and Budbrooke

This walk begins with a delightful canal-side stroll, passes through some attractive woodland, visits a typical Warwickshire village church, and then returns to the starting point along another pleasant section of the canal.

Start: Hatton Locks (GR243669)
Distance: 7 miles; shorter option 5½ miles.
Maps: Landranger 151; Pathfinder 976.
Parking: Pay and Display car park at lock 42 on the Grand Union Canal. This is reached by turning off the A4117 Solihull-Warwick road some 200 yards east of The Waterman public house. (*Before you leave the car park, note the time at which the gates are closed.*)
Public Transport: Trains between Birmingham and Warwick stop at Hatton Station. From the station walk up the station approach to the road and then start reading from ★ below.
Refreshments: The Waterman (access from the canal at bridge 54).

FROM the car park cross the canal at bridge No. 54, viewing some of the magnificent Hatton Locks to left and to right. Turn right and walk along the towpath for about 1½ miles, soon passing a picnic area, the Hatton Canal Shop (a converted stable for the horses which worked the towpaths) and continuing through a lovely tree-lined cutting,.

On the 145 miles of the Grand Union Canal between London and Birmingham, there are 150 locks. Of these, 21 are to be found in the two miles of Hatton Locks, the water level changing by nearly 150 feet. You will, on this walk, pass 20 of these locks (which were built in 1810 and widened in 1934). Remains of the original narrow locks can be seen in the lock-side weirs.

Looking out for herons as you go, reach bridge 56, and, immediately beyond it, climb up steps to the road. Turn right to cross the railway.

★ *Rail travellers join here, turning left from the station approach.*

Follow the road through the village. Soon cross the noisy M40 and at the T-junction turn left (signed Haseley 2¼), passing the decorated gates and the stables of Fingerpost Meadow. The hedges hereabouts are loaded in autumn with purple sloes and with the red fruits of dog rose, hawthorn, white bryony and guelder rose.

These fruits form a valuable part of the diets of birds, particularly members of the thrush family. Our residents (blackbirds and song- and mistle-thrushes) are joined in mid-October by large invasions of fieldfares and redwings which migrate from Scandinavia to take advantage of this bounty. When the fieldfares are here, you will, no doubt, hear their familiar, repeated 'chack-chack' call.

Follow the winding road as it swings round, back towards the motorway. At the next T-junction, turn left (signed Hatton 1¼) to cross the motorway again. Having done this immediately turn right over a stile and walk along a concrete drive parallel to the motorway. Very shortly after passing a radio tower, turn left over a stile, then turn right to walk with wooden palings on your right. Reaching a stile, cross this and follow the path as it hugs the north-east edge of a ribbon of woodland. In early summer it is richly carpeted with wild flowers – but look out for holes in the path! The sounds of the motorway soon diminish.

Reaching a stile, cross this onto a drive and turn right, then immediately left to pass Wilderness Cottage. As you walk on, imagine the solitude of this area before the intrusion of the motorway! Pass the buildings of Grove Park Farm and soon gently descend past woodland to reach a metalled road.

From this junction, you will see, in the distance straight ahead, a grey water tower which stands on Montgomery Avenue, Hampton Magna. World War II hero, Field Marshall Viscount Montgomery of Alamein, popularly known as 'Monty', became a national hero after his decisive victory over the Afrika Korps at El Alamein in 1942 and his pursuit of the Germans across Libya and Tunisia. He was the last Commander-in-Chief of the Royal Warwickshire Regiment which was, until the

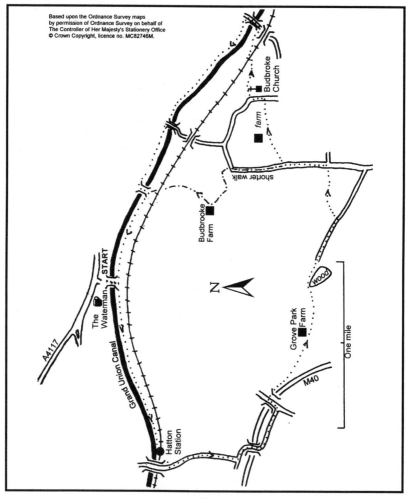

name disappeared in 1963 when the regiment was amalgamated with others, based at Budbrooke Barracks. All that remains of the barracks is this water tower, the remainder of the area having been redeveloped to form Hampton Magna.

Turn right onto the road, pass a couple of houses and then walk along past a double row of poplars. About 170 yards beyond the last of the poplars, turn left through a gap in the hedge by a multi-waymarked post and walk forward about 60 yards to a large oak which is waymarked on its far side. Immediately beyond the oak, go through a hedge gap and then swing to the right to pass through another hedge gap then to walk with a hedge on your right.

Follow the farm track as it curves to the right and, as you go, see the lofty tower of St Mary's Church, Warwick way ahead of you. Reaching a road at a road junction, turn left, passing 'Except for Access' signs. Stay on this lane for about 500 yards until you reach a giant oak just before the metal railings of a small road bridge.

The longer and shorter walks separate here. For the longer walk now continue reading from ★ below.

For the **shorter** walk continue along the road for about a quarter of a mile where the lane bends abruptly to the right. Here, go straight ahead on a farm lane which goes left and right to pass to the right of barns at Budbrooke Farm. Just before the farmhouse, turn right onto a broad strip of grassland. At the end of this, enter a field and go half left, aiming more-or-less in the direction of a bell tower of the old Hatton Hospital, which is evident on the skyline. Pass under a railway bridge and walk on, through scrubland, to reach and cross a concrete footbridge - number 53 - beyond which you turn left to reach the towpath and rejoin the main route at ❂ on page 54.

★ Continuing the longer walk, cross the waymarked stile by the side of the giant oak. Walk forward with a watery ditch on your left and about halfway along the field cross the ditch and go right over a stile by the side of a gateway. Continue with a hedge on the right, Budbrooke church coming into view ahead. Cross a stile – this area can be rather muddy at times – and walk on, initially with the hedge on your right. Then, as the hedge swings away to the right, bear slightly left up to the top of the rise ahead, aiming for a pair of red-brick cottages.

When you reach the point where the hedge gives way to a wire fence, cross a stile beside a gate and turn right along a rough lane. At a T-junction turn left and in 75 yards enter the churchyard of Budbrooke Church. Here you see a weather vane topped with the badge of the Royal Warwickshire Regiment and later pass graves of members of the regiment.

The first incumbent of the parish of St Michael's, Budbroke was Ric de Bradewell in 1273. Though St Mary's in Warwick was the regimental church of the RWR, St Michael's, being the local church to the barracks, was used for company church parades.

Walk to the left of the church tower and leave the block-paved path here to follow a gravel path to a wicket gate and a stile. From the stile go half-right to reach another stile in the far fence. Cross this – an awkward one – and walk forward, initially with the hedge on your right, but then, as it swings away, continue forward to the far left corner of the field. Go through a gate and pass under the railway.

Turn right along the field margin which runs parallel with the adjacent railway embankment. Follow the boundary as it swings left and cross a concrete bridge, then swing left to cross a stile about 10 yards to the left of a gate. Reaching a road turn left along this, crossing a bridge and then shortly crossing another over the canal.

Beyond this bridge, continue along the road for about 100 yards, then turn 180° left by the gate of The Coach House to take a path back to the canal (*though there is a well-used but unofficial cut down to the canal just over the bridge*). Turn right along the excellently-maintained towpath, passing lock No. 27, and walk for about 1½ miles *en route* passing beneath bridge 52 which, though called Ugly Bridge, seems little different from the others!

❂ *At bridge No. 53 the shorter route rejoins the main walk.*

Reaching lock 42 and bridge 54 you are back at the car park. For refreshment The Waterman is close by. Cross the stile to the left of the white house and walk up the field to reach the pub.

If you have travelled by train now continue reading from the start of the chapter.

12

Henley-in-Arden and a Reminder of Long-Forgotten Crimes

A short round from the pretty township of Henley-in-Arden, passing the scene of a grim story.

Start: Henley-in-Arden Guildhall (GR151661)
Distance: 6½ miles, shorter option 5 miles.
Parking: Roadsides on the High Street, Henley-in-Arden on the A3400 but note that there are time restrictions on most days of the week. A free car park is located at the south end of the town, off Warwick Road (A4189).
Maps: Landranger 151 and (just) 150 ; Pathfinder 975.
Public Transport: Trains on the Birmingham-Stratford-upon-Avon line stop at Henley-in-Arden. *If arriving by train cross the footbridge to the west side of the station and then start reading from ★ below.* Stagecoach bus service X20 also connects Birmingham with Stratford-upon-Avon.
Refreshments: Public houses and eating houses are abundant in Henley-in-Arden.

THE walk starts outside the fifteenth century Guildhall. Walk northwards (in the direction of Birmingham) along High Street to Station Road, using the pelican crossing *en route*. Walk up Station Road for about 300 yards and, immediately before the station, cross the tracks via a footbridge.

★ *Rail travellers join here.*

At the other side, take an immediate right turn and follow an (initially) enclosed footpath alongside the railway line. Stay close to the railway until, about half a mile after crossing a lane, you reach the first tee of Crocketts Manor golf course. Immediately beyond this, turn left and walk up a very slight incline, veering right and left just before you reach the club house. Beyond the car parks, swing right and walk on with houses on your left and tennis courts on your right. Soon after you reach a small pool, continue ahead with the hedge on your left.

On reaching a large ornamental lake, go with (and stay with) the hedge as it diverts to the left and, about 100 yards after walking beneath overhead wires, cross a stile. Proceed two-thirds left across the ensuing field, aiming for a gate on the far side of a rusty-red barn. On reaching a lane, turn left and, in about 70 yards, leave the lane to join a footpath between a white house and some red-brick ones. Having passed between the houses, walk on along a track to reach and cross a stile beside a gateway. Continue along a muddy lane for about 70 yards until, shortly before a wicket gate, you turn right, soon to reach a stile. Cross this, turn left and walk on following the field margin with the hedge on your left. You soon walk past Hall End Farm.

According to Vivian Bird's "Bird's Eye View: the Midlands", in the early 1800s this farm was occupied by the Booth family whose two sons, John and William, both came to macabre ends. John was murdered here at Hall End Farm, William being accused of the crime but acquitted. However, William was later convicted of forgery, then a capital crime. He was executed at Stafford Jail – at the third attempt, the rope being insecure the first time and the scaffold mechanism having failed on the second.

Leaving the farm behind, continue with the hedge on your left until, when you reach a patch of woodland, you turn left to reach a lane onto which you turn right. Continue along the lane for about 150 yards when you cross a tiny footbridge and stile on your left. Walk straight up the field to cross a stile in the hedge-elbow ahead. After continuing up the incline, enter, by way of another stile, the graveyard of Ullenhall Old Chapel.

This old building, restored in 1962, is the chancel of the original Ullenhall church. Several tablets record the names of members of the Knight family, these referred to in a note on the Winged Spur, Ullenhall on Walk 10. This Chapel was near the centre of the village until most of the population was destroyed by the plague. A new village developed half-a-mile or so to the west. The church of St Mary's, which was also visited on Walk 10, is now the main church of the village.

If the door is unlocked you may like to look around the chapel. It contains a number of features of interest including some medieval decorated floor tiles in front of the altar steps and a memorial to Francis Throckmorton who was granted the manorship of Ullenhall in 1553.

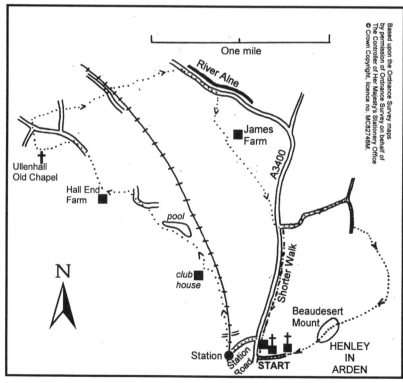

56

Leave the churchyard by the gate on the west side and bear right across a gravelled parking space by Old Chapel Cottage to a stile. Cross this, walk on for a few yards and then turn right and aim for a stile in the far bottom corner of the field near a red house. Having crossed this stile, you are at road junction. Opposite you is a single-track road. Walk up this road for about 10 yards and, before the red house, cross a stile on your right. Follow an evergreen hedge for a few yards to another stile.

Cross this and then walk half-left across the next field, passing the corner of paddock railings, to reach a gate to the left of tree-shrouded farm buildings. Having passed through this gate, go very slightly left across a lane to cross a stile. Walk across a rough paddock to another stile and then, bearing slightly right, continue up the slope, aiming for a clump of trees at the top. On approaching the field boundary, you will see two stiles ahead of you. Cross the *right* hand one and walk down the incline to cross a stile at the far right-hand corner of the field near a white cottage. A winding, enclosed path soon leads to a lane.

Turn left and, in 20 yards, go over a stile on the right. This is soon followed by another stile which leads to the railway track. Cross this *with great care – approaching trains are not easily heard* – and negotiate the stile on the far side. Now go half-right to another stile by an electricity post – not the one equipped with a transformer and standing near a black-and-white house, but the next one to the right. Cross this stile and go three-quarters left to cross a stile beneath a lonely oak. Now proceed half-right down the slope, aiming to the left of houses.

On reaching a road, turn right and walk ahead, accompanied for some of the way by the young River Alne. 200 yards past the driveway of the last house of this group, pass through a gate on the right and, turning half-left and passing an isolated burred oak, reach the hedge at the far side of the field. Now turn right and follow the hedge up the field. 70 yards after crossing a three-barred, wooden horse-jump, pass a pool and bear left and follow the hedge up past James Farm. The sky ahead of you is criss-crossed by numerous wires and cables.

At the top of the slope, follow the hedge as it makes a right-angle turn and goes down in the direction of a pylon. Near the pylon, cross a stile and continue down a gravel-covered drive which ultimately delivers you onto the A3400, Birmingham to Stratford road. Here turn right and walk along the pavement until you reach the turn for Buckley Green. Cautiously cross the road.

Here the longer and shorter walks separate. For the longer walk continue from ★ below.

To shorten your walk and return directly to Henley rejoin the pavement and continue along the A3400 – pondering, maybe, how much busier this busy thoroughfare must have been before the construction of the M40. If you have travelled by train turn right into Station Road shortly before the Guildhall.

★ Continuing the **longer** walk turn left along the road for Buckley Green until after about half a mile you reach a T-junction. Turn right here and after passing the remains of a bridge of a dismantled railway immediately take a footpath on the left that leads into a field. Go straight forward across the field and through a gateway.

Now ascend the hill ahead, swinging right as you do so to reach a horse jump about 100 yards to the right of the top right hand corner of the field. Cross this and go forward, following the fine ridge path until you reach a gate and another horse jump. Go forward a few yards and then swing right, downhill.

After passing the remains of an old hedge the path ascends Beaudesert Mount, the site of a Norman castle. From the highest point descend (west) to reach a road via a kissing gate beside the Church of St Nicholas. Follow the road, crossing the River Alne, into the town.

If you have travelled by train cross the road, turn right and go along Shallowford Court, just past the White Swan. Follow this through the car park and then left along a tarmac track. Pass Swan Croft and continue along the track into Station Road where the station is on your left.

13

Ups and Downs around Abberley and Great Witley

This walk, the hilliest in the book, visits west Worcestershire, notable for its peace and quiet and for its exquisite views.

Start: Great Witley (GR 757657).
Distance: 6 miles; shorter option 5 miles (The diversion to Great Witley Court adds nearly two miles to these distances.)
Maps: Landranger 138; Pathfinder 973.
Parking: Public car park in front of Great Witley Parish Hall on A443 opposite junction of B4197.
Public Transport: Very limited bus service 758 Worcester/Tenbury Wells stops at Great Witley.
Refreshments: The Manor Arms at Abberley Village.
Places of interest: Witley Court and Church. *(Telephone 01299 896636 for details.)*
! When planning this walk, bear in mind that its hilly nature makes it more demanding, and so will take more time, than other walks of similar length in this book.

FROM the car park, cross the road and, to the right of the old village school with its Tudor-style chimneys and pretty barge boards, walk down the B4197. After a little over 100 yards, join a tarmacked drive which veers off to the right between evergreen trees. After passing to the right of a pool, go through a gate and, in less than 10 yards, go through a muddy gateway on your right and walk on, half left, to reach a double stile, passing hawthorn bushes bearing mistletoe on your left.

Mistletoe is a partial parasite. It relies on its host plant for its supply of minerals and water but, being green, it is capable of making its own sugars by photosynthesis. A host of legends are associated with this plant, one being that, originally a tree itself, it was condemned to this dependency since its wood was used to make Christ's cross at Calvary. It was also considered to have magical powers and was a favourite of early herbalists.

Continue on the same bearing up the next field where, at the top left-hand corner, you cross a stile and walk ahead, now following a wire fence. The adjacent goose farm was visited at a recent Christmastide by two well-known, female television chefs who travel by motor cycle combination! The next stile leads to a lane onto which you turn left and, in 75 yards, reach another lane leading off to the right. Near the far corner of this junction, take a waymarked path veering off into the woodland. This path soon joins a forest road as it gradually climbs Woodbury Hill. As you approach the summit, just beyond a stand of dark conifers, take a right turn at the first waymark post and walk 150 yards or so up to a cairn.

59

The cairn, with the initials JFCB, marks the highest point on the hill (904 feet). Undergrowth obscures remnants of the earthworks of a camp which was a stronghold even before Roman times. Rather later, in the fifteenth century, Owain Glyndwr's army was camped here keeping watch on that of Henry IV which was entrenched on Abberley Hill. There was no bloodshed since Glyndwr and his followers, after eight days, retreated into Wales.

Retrace your steps to the waymark post, turn right and walk for 10 yards or so to another waymark post. Across the track from this is yet another waymark (nailed onto a young sycamore tree) which directs you to a thin path which slants down through trees. You will soon have a fine, end-on view of the Malvern Hills to the south. Passing splendid, old sweet chestnut trees, you reach a wider track onto which you turn right.

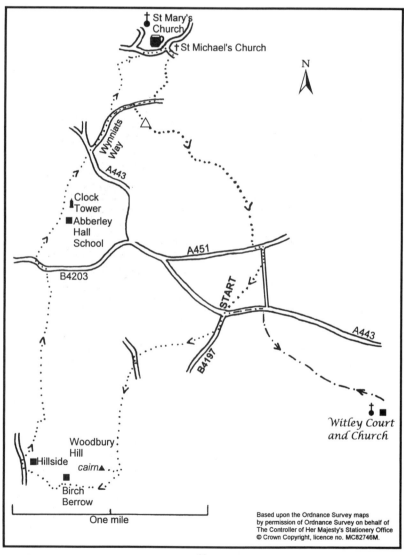

St Mary's Church

St Michael's Church

N

Wynniats Way

A443

Clock Tower

Abberley Hall School

A451

B4203

START

A451

A443

B4197

Witley Court and Church

Woodbury Hill

Hillside

cairn

Birch Berrow

One mile

Based upon the Ordnance Survey maps by permission of Ordnance Survey on behalf of The Controller of Her Majesty's Stationery Office © Crown Copyright, licence no. MC82746M.

Approaching Abberley

This track soon angles down to the left, but you stay with the wire fence at the end of which you turn right over a stile. Ignoring the stile which is immediately on your left, walk ahead on a clear track on the edge of woodland. In just over 200 yards, you reach a farm gate to the left of which is a stile. After crossing it, go half right to walk past a ha-ha which gives the inhabitants of Birch Berrow magnificent views over the Teme Valley and beyond.

Continue with the boundary on your right to cross a stile onto a drive along which you turn left. This leads to a junction of farm tracks. Go half-left for about 20 yards to find, beside the second farm gate, a stile which you cross. Now go half left down a steepish grassy meadow. As you go, ignore a stile on the left (halfway down) and make for the stile at the bottom which leads into gloomy coniferous woodland where, in autumn, a profusion of fungi may be seen. The path then continues downwards, soon angling off to the right and, later, to the left. After crossing a stile, follow the (now clearer) path's meandering course until you come near to houses. Via a short corridor of young evergreen shrubs, walk to the drive of one of these houses (Hillside) and pass through its gate to reach a lane. The Clee Hills may be visible ahead of you.

Turn right and, immediately past the houses, take a permissive path to the right and walk up into the wood where you bear left onto a clear track and begin a slow climb. Taking the advice of a waymark post after about 350 yards, turn sharply to the right and walk on for about 50 yards when, above you on your left beneath a yew tree, you see a stile on the horizon. Walk up to this stile but *do not cross it*. However, just before it, take the path (the Worcestershire Way) going left which follows the top of the ridge. Crossing two stiles *en route*, stay on this path, admiring, on clear days, a fine panorama over a part of rural England of which we should be proud.

When, just after passing over a third stile, the Abberley clock tower comes into view, take a diagonal path down to your left in the general direction of the tower. The path curves steeply down to a stile (near white-walled houses) beyond which you turn right onto a lane which soon reaches a road (B4203). Here turn left, carefully cross the road and walk ahead for about 130 yards to the driveway of Abberley Hall School.

Walk between its elaborate, sandstone gateposts and through its heavy, ornamental gates to join a bridleway which skirts playing fields to reach the school. Just beyond the school buildings, ignore a footpath going off to the left, but continue on the bridleway, following the blue markers, soon passing to the left of the clock tower (no public access). Look out for deer behind a high fence on the left.

Abberley and the Clock Tower

62

Called Jones's Folly after John Joseph Jones who built it in 1883, the tower is over 160 feet high and originally housed a carillon of twenty-one bells. Although few remain, there are enough to chime every quarter hour.

On reaching a busy road (A443), cross with care to Wynniatts Way and walk up this steep road for about a quarter of a mile until, about 15 yards past a house called The Beeches, you join a public footpath going off to the left (signposted Bank Lane).

*If you wish to take the **shorter** route which misses out Abberley Village, walk on up the hill for a further 120 yards to join the main route at ★ on page 64, just beyond a house called Brackenthwaite.*

Continuing on the **longer** route, walk to the top right hand corner of the field to find and cross a stile at the corner of green railings which surround covered reservoirs. Follow a rather indistinct path which twists its way from the stile through bracken towards the top of the ridge where, by two double-trunked oak trees, you join another meandering path which leads very steeply down the other side. Nearing the end, cross a stile and soon go over a crossing track. Near the bottom, just after passing between newly planted trees and beneath triple electricity wires, you reach a field, directly across which your path goes.

When you reach the boundary fence on the other side, turn right to walk ahead to a green lane which, in just under 150 yards, delivers you to a metal kissing gate. Pass through this to a road onto which you turn right. Walk along this road towards Abberley village, noticing, on your left, the 'new' church (St Mary's) which was built, reputedly for £7000, in the early 1850s to replace the structurally unsound, old church (St Michael's) which you will have a chance to visit shortly. On reaching the centre of the village, straight ahead of you is St Michael's.

The twelfth century Norman building was abandoned in the middle of the last century. The chancel, all that had survived from the old church, was sensitively restored in the 1960s and is again in active use. The Saxon tomb cover, outside, leaning against the west wall, is of great antiquity, whilst the old bell, just inside the door, was brought from the north of England and given to the parish by Rev. John Blamyre when he was appointed Rector in 1514.

On leaving the church, cross the road and enter a narrow lane opposite (signed Wynniatts Way). You are now on the Worcestershire Way again and its green pear waymarks will assist your navigation. After 100 yards, turn left soon to cross a stile, 10 yards beyond which you turn right to enter a paddock. Walk up the grassy slope aiming for a wooden electricity post which is just to the left of a house. Cross a stile a few yards beyond the post and continue up the incline, soon to negotiate another stile which leads into a field.

Now continue your ascent, hugging the right-hand boundary. The steepness of the slope will, no doubt, encourage you to stop from time to time to turn round and admire the panoramic view of north Worcestershire. On reaching the corner of the field, cross a stile on your right and continue your climb on a clear path which wanders through woodland. At the top of an eighteen-step staircase you reach a road (Wynniatts Way) onto which you turn right. At the top of the incline, climb the stile on your left (signed Worcestershire Way North), here to be joined by those who have used the shorter route.

★ You resume your ascent on a clear path between the trees, a path which, at the time of going to print, was still well waymarked. When you reach a trig point, you can be sure that, apart from minor undulations, your day's climbing is at an end!

As explained on page 44, trig points are now redundant. This one, atop Flagstaff Wood, was adopted by Bournville Walking Club in 1994 and is maintained by its members. You are now 928 feet above sea level, the highest point on the walk.

Continue ahead on the Worcestershire Way which follows the top of the ridge and may be somewhat overgrown in places, particularly in summer. You stay on the path, initially alongside a corroded iron fence, for about half-a-mile and, since the exit path may easily be missed, the route will be described in stages. After 500 yards or so, the path veers a little to the right and begins to descend more markedly. About 200 yards further on, you will see on your left a gnarled old yew close to a huge, ancient ash which has several young trunks growing from its base.

About 200 yards past these trees, at (vandals permitting) the second waymark, take a thin path off to the right by an ivy-clad, elder tree. The path soon widens and becomes clearer. Continue downwards between the trees, crossing over the farm track of a fruit farm as you go. Ultimately, you reach a road (the A451) onto which you turn left. In 65 yards, turn right onto the B4197. Continue down this road and, in 400 yards, if you do not intend to visit Witley Court go through a hedge gap on the right to use a diagonal path across the field to reach the car park.

To reach Witley Court, continue ahead to the road junction where, with care, you cross the A443 to join a rough lane which leads, after nearly three-quarters of a mile, to Witley Court and Church.

Witley Court, severely damaged by fire in 1937, is now being gradually restored by English Heritage, parts of the ruins being open to the public with good audio guide facilities. The adjacent church, consecrated in 1735, has been described as 'the finest baroque church in the country'. Its ceiling paintings, painted glass windows and gold-leaved plasterwork are truly breathtaking and make the trek up the drive well worthwhile.

Retrace your steps down to the main road and, on reaching it, turn left and walk for nearly 300 yards back to your starting place.

14
Ombersley and the River Severn

This walk takes you along the banks of Britain's longest river and also through some of Worcestershire's leafy lanes.

Start: Ombersley church (GR845635).
Distance: 9 miles
Maps: Landranger 150; Pathfinder 974.
Parking: Roadsides by the church on the road which runs south from the roundabout in Ombersley village.
Public Transport: MRW service 303 Kidderminster/Worcester stops in Ombersley.
Refreshments: The Crown and Sandys, the Kings Arms and the Cross Keys in Ombersley; the Wharf Inn and the Holt Fleet Inn on the Severn near Holt Bridge.

WALK southwards from the church down the road which, before the new A449T was built a short distance away, carried heavy traffic through the village.

On a house opposite the Kings Arms you may notice, high up above the pavement, a tablet which commemorates the founding of a charity school by Richard Lloyd in 1729. Further on, you see delightful old black-and-white cottages.

After about half a mile and just past Sinton cottages on the left, about 50 yards before no-through-road signs, turn right onto a footpath to Turn Mill, joining the Wychavon Way. Continue directly ahead, crossing Ombersley Park and soon gaining a glimpse of Ombersley Court through trees on your right. To the south you may see the Malvern Hills. The path then skirts woodland within which are fishponds. When the major pond comes into view, a waymark diverts you to walk close beside the pond for a few yards.

Just beyond the pond, the path slopes down, soon crossing a plank bridge and joining a rough, farm track onto which you turn left. Follow this Wychavon-waymarked track as it meanders along, finally petering out, in about 100 yards, into a well-trodden path entering woodland again. Follow this path as it climbs gently and then begins to descend quite sharply, ignoring a minor path which soon branches off to the left.

A stile at the bottom of the incline leads to a field in which you walk ahead to a waymark post near the river bank. Here turn right, still following the Wychavon Way, walking upstream with the River Severn on your left and, maybe, passing the time of day with anglers and passing boat-people. After about three-quarters of a mile you reach Holt Fleet bridge.

Locally abundant in summer and early autumn, the tall, pink-flowered plant on the river bank is "policemen's helmet" or "Himalayan balsam". A close relative of our potted "Busy Lizzies", this plant was introduced from the Himalayas about 150 years ago. When its ripe fruits are touched, they explode, throwing the seeds several feet away from the parent plant. But if you try to investigate, don't fall into the river!

Pass under the metal-arched bridge (designed by Thomas Telford and built in 1828) and, in a couple of hundred yards, reach Holt Lock which allows river traffic to circumnavigate the rapids on the far side of the river. This is one of a series of locks which makes the Severn navigable for the 43 miles between Gloucester to Stourport. Continue on the riverside path, enjoying the company of swans, moorhen, coot, mallard and other wildlife as you go.

After about another mile, as you admire some of the waterside homes on the far bank, cross a stile close to the river and walk along a roped-off pathway past moored boats, a pretty pool complete with water-lilies, bullrushes and a weeping willow and the attractive garden of Mutton Hall. Just after Mutton Hall, go through a wicket gate to join a wide bridleway on the edges of which, in the warmer months, comfrey (more fully described on page 9) is abundant.

After about 500 yards or so, follow this track as it swings to the right away from the river and takes you away from the Severn Way on which you have walked since Holt Fleet bridge. You begin a gentle climb and just before meeting woodland on your left, you turn left, go down to a plank bridge and enter a field and walk along its margin with the woodland on your right. Continue until, just after a white house, you veer right to join a rough,

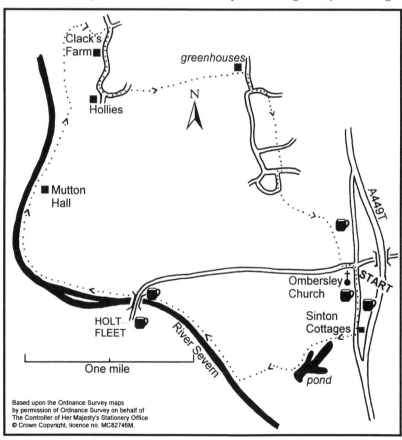

gravel-surfaced road which wanders up through trees to reach a road junction. Here you turn right and walk along the narrow lane soon coming to Clack's Farm on your right.

Viewers may recall a popular television gardening programme which was regularly broadcast some time ago from Clack's Farm and which was introduced by the late Arthur Billett.

Leaving Clack's Farm behind, you follow the lane as it twists its way, this way and that, passing a pets' cemetery (several graves had fresh flowers on them on a recent visit), until you turn left at the road junction by 'Hollies'. In about 175 yards, having ignored the first path going off to the right, you take a path (number 46) on your right. After passing through a small area of rough ground, proceed with the tall hedge on your right. After the first stile, go slightly left up an incline to another stile. After crossing this, walk slightly left up the field aiming for some tall trees on the horizon.

Beneath these trees, a sandy-surfaced tractor track leads on in the same direction. Having passed a large greenhouse (possibly, from its appearance, due for demolition) and a row of conifers, on your left, you soon reach a road into which you turn right. After about 100 yards, turn left at a junction and walk down the incline for about 150 yards and, opposite a tall holly hedge, turn right through a signposted gap in a sandstone-and-brick wall. Walk on slightly to the left, across the field, aiming for the near end of a tall hedge. Having reached this, walk ahead on its right side. The hedge ends after a little over 100 yards here, you bear slightly left for about ten yards and then join a gently-curving path with a short, sharp upward slope at your right hand. This finally delivers you onto a roadway.

Turn left into this and, in ten yards or so, turn right over another stile. Walk ahead with the hedge on your right and continue until you reach another lane with a small pool directly ahead of you. Here turn right and walk up the lane for about 30 yards and then turn left into another lane. After passing a black-and-white house (another one called The Hollies!), continue ahead onto a tarmacked bridleway with a 'no-through-road' sign beside it.

Just after passing under the second line of triple electricity cables, the track veers right but you take a narrow path passing through a hedge up to the left and follow this path down a field as it hugs the hedge on your right. When the hedge swings to the right, continue ahead through horticultural land until, just before the first house, you turn right and follow a well-defined path which leads into a road (Apple Tree Walk) which soon reaches the main road through Ombersley village. Here turn left and then, at the roundabout, right to retrace your steps to your starting place.

The existing church in Ombersley, built in 1825, is dedicated to St Andrew and is believed to be the fourth church on the site. The chancel of its immediate predecessor, dedicated to St Ambrose in the early 1600s, is still present in the churchyard and houses memorials to the Sandys family. The bells from St Ambrose's and some of its original stonework are now installed in St Andrews within which you may be impressed with the lofty main aisle. At the top of the south aisle, the spacious Sandys family pew has its own fireplace over which is a tablet recording the sadness of the family at the death of a nine-year-old daughter in 1854.

15
A Circuit from Wootton Wawen

This, the longest walk in the book, explores a quiet wedge of pretty countryside between the busy Alcester and Stratford Roads.

Start: The Bull's Head in Wootton Wawen (GR151632), a hostelry which dates from 1387.
Distance: 11 miles; shorter option 8 miles.
Maps: Landranger 150/151; Pathfinder 975.
Parking: The A3400 is unsuitable for parking but space should be found on road sides on the B4089 (to Alcester).
Public Transport: Stagecoach service X50 (Birmingham,Stratford, Oxford) (join walk at the Bull's Head) and rail services on the Birmingham to Stratford line (Join walk at ★ below)
Refreshments: The Bull's Head, Wootton Wawen.

WALK away from the village on Alcester Road (B4089) and, where this turns off to the left, continue straight ahead on Wawensmere Road, noticing the interesting Tollgate Cottage on the corner. Staying on Wawensmere Road, pass under the railway bridge on the façade of which is a Staffordshire knot, the logo of the Darlaston company which built the bridge in 1906.

★ *Rail travellers join here.*

Continue up the incline, being rewarded in springtime with a good display of daffodils near its summit. This road, though wide, is not generally very busy and should present no hazards but, since wide roads sometimes attract wild drivers, take care! Continue on the road until, about three-quarters of a mile after leaving the Bull's Head and about 150 yards past the first entrance to Elmhurst Farm (just before a white house on the right), cross a stile on your *left*. As you walk across the field, you will see, ahead of you, three large chicken houses. Walk between the one on the left and the middle one and, on emerging, veer very slightly left and right to join a concrete-surfaced drive which leads you down to the left of more buildings.

At the end of this drive, again veer slightly left and right to continue down the incline on a grassy track. Pass through a hedge gap at the bottom of the slope and then go half right on a clear path diagonally up the next field. At the end of this, cross a stile and walk on with the hedge on your right, noticing the various designs of horse-jump which interrupt these hedges. Cross another stile and continue forward. The next two stiles lead you into and out of a small spinney-plus-pool. Walk on, maintaining the same heading to reach and cross a stile which is preceded by an awkward cross-barrier. A short track leads to a road onto which you turn right, soon to enter the hamlet of Shelfield. At the first road junction, the two routes separate.

For the shorter route continue reading from the following paragraph. For the longer walk read from ✪ on page 69

Following the **shorter** route, here turn left (signposted Shelfield Green) and walk ahead on this twisty lane for nearly half-a-mile to a house called Mearsecroft. Immediately after the house, go through a gateway on the right and walk straight across the field in the direction of a three-storey house. Cross the stream ahead on a tractor path and follow this for about 25 yards up an incline then turn left to continue with the stream on your left. Passing various pheasant-feeding devices as you go, stay near the meandering stream.

Meeting a facing hedge, go right with this for a few yards, then go through a gap in it and over a narrow plank bridge. Continue on your original heading and when you reach a road, go left and immediately right to join an enclosed bridleway, passing the intriguingly-named Tut's Cottage and the adjoining Tut's Castle on your right.

Residents of neither of these houses know the origin of the names. One theory is that the Tut family lived here at one time. Another is that a 'tut-man' (a kind of itinerant piece-worker, who went from place to place doing specified jobs for an agreed fee) was based here. Or is there another, more interesting, explanation?

This bridleway can become extremely muddy. *If it proves impassable, go back to the houses, turn left and walk up to a road junction. Turn left to join the main route at ✿ on page 71.* If you continue on the bridleway, at its end go through a gateway and turn right passing a stile on the right , here rejoining the main route at ✳ on page 71.)

❍ Following the **longer** route now continue ahead through Shelfield. About 400 yards after passing the turn for Wawensmoor, fork right onto a rough lane, soon concreted. On reaching a group of dwellings (including

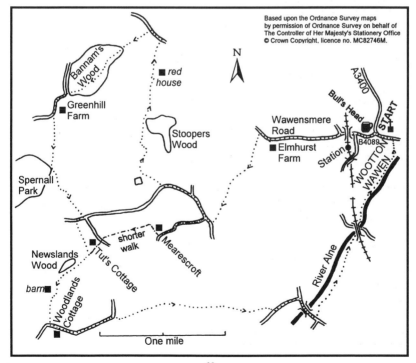

Based upon the Ordnance Survey maps by permission of Ordnance Survey on behalf of The Controller of Her Majesty's Stationery Office © Crown Copyright, licence no. MC82746M.

N

Bannam's Wood

red house

Greenhill Farm

Stoopers Wood

Wawensmere Road

Bull's Head

A3400

START

B4089

Elmhurst Farm

Station

WOOTTON WAWEN

Spernall Park

shorter walk

Tut's Cottage

Mearescroft

River Alne

Newslands Wood

barn

Woodlands Cottage

One mile

Partridge Barn), turn right onto a tractor track. When, after about 100 yards, this track swings off to the left, walk straight ahead with the hedge on your right. You may, as you walk through this field, flush partridges and pheasants and realise why so many of the houses that you have just passed bear the names of game-birds.

At the field's end, turn left and continue with a narrow spinney on your right. Immediately past the spinney pass through a hedge gap on the right and walk ahead alongside the hedge as it winds its way up a gradual incline. You will, as you go, pass several ancient, burred oaks which, though in various stages of decay and ravaged by woodworm, still manage to hang onto life. At the top of the incline, where the hedge swings left, cross a fence stile and a subsequent ditch and walk on, initially with Stoopers Wood on your right.

As you approach a red-brick house, you will have, on your left hand side, a row of young poplars (interspersed with other species) and, closer to your right hand, you will enjoy an impressive row of daffodils in spring. Pass through a wicket gate and continue towards the house for just over 50 yards. Here, walk through a hedge gap on your left, this protected by a permanently propped-open gate. Now continue on your former heading up the slope with the hedge and, later, the red house and other buildings on your right. Walk on, arrow-straight, until you reach a lane onto which you turn left. After about 150 yards cross a stile on the left, pass through a small patch of newly-planted trees and then begin a gradual ascent with the hedge on your right.

You are now on the Heart of England Way and will, apart form a brief excursion into Bannam's Wood, stay on it for the next three miles. This long-distance path runs from Cannock Chase to Bourton-on-the-Water, in total about 100 miles.

At the top of the steep part of the slope, you come to a stile. (Here, you temporarily leave the Heart of England Way. You may wish to pause to regain your breath and to savour good views over the wooded Warwickshire countryside.) Do not cross the stile ahead of you but turn right just before it and then continue on your original bearing on an enclosed path which soon leads, via another stile, into Bannam's Wood.

Bannam's Wood is designated as a Site of Special Scientific Interest and, if you have a dog with you, you are asked to keep it on its leash to prevent disturbing the wildlife.

The path wanders through the wood but is reasonably distinct. Soon, having walked past a redundant stile, you come to a patch of conifers, immediately before which your path passes to the right of the skeletal remains of an old farm cart. The path soon begins to descend and later joins a tractor track which can be muddy and slippery at times. After ignoring a branch sharp left, reach a T-junction. Here go left and continue downwards until you reach a lane. Turn left and follow the twisting lane for 300 yards or so, rejoining the Heart of England Way *en route*.

Immediately past the ornamental gates of the former Greenhill Farm (now 'Kalium Products'), pass through a metal gate on your left and then go half-right down the field, i.e. walking *away from* the railings around Greenhill Farm. At the bottom of the incline, cross a stile and footbridge beyond which the path leads up a slope between brambles, wild roses and blackthorn. Cross a stile at the top and continue with the hedge on your left.

About 80 yards past the next stile, the path veers very slightly left and crosses the field ahead, aiming towards a prominent hillock called Round Hill. After passing through a gateway on the immediate left of more woodland (Spernall Park), turn left and follow the field margin until you reach a complex of two stiles and a wicket gate. Go through the gate and cross the stile immediately ahead of you and then walk on, with the hedge on your left as it gradually curves to the left. After two more stiles, a double stile leads to a road onto which you turn right.

✿ *Those who have detoured to escape mud on the shorter route may join you here!*

After about 75 yards, cross a stile on your left. Walk on with the hedge on your right, noticing a white house ahead of you which is Tut's Cottage (mentioned on the shorter option above). When the hedge swings away to the right, stay on the same bearing until you reach a stile. Cross this and turn right.

✳ *Here you are joined by those who have stayed on the shorter route.*

Walk ahead towards woodland (Newslands Wood) and continue round its left margin until a gateway leads you on a clear track up through bluebell woodland. Emerging at its top end, the track begins a descent and then passes in front of a barn. Soon, the track swings left and continues downwards, affording good panoramic views ahead *en route*. At the bottom of the track, you join a lane onto which you turn left and walk ahead.

In the autumn, having seen so many blackberries on this walk, your thoughts may have drifted towards preserves. Have no fear for you may soon be able to purchase some of Mrs Busby's range as you pass Woodlands Cottage, the next dwelling on the right. Highly recommended – they're delicious!

Continue on this lane as it swings left, ascends an incline past farms and barn-conversions. At the next bend, where a post box faces you, as the road swings to the left you bear right then, in about 35 yards, veer left on to a bridleway. (This runs in an easterly direction for just over a mile. It provides easy walking, on a relatively good surface and down a slight incline, and it follows the Monarch's Way.)

This long distance path (610 miles in total) follows the route taken by Charles II after his defeat at the Battle of Worcester in 1651. Hotly pursued by Cromwell's forces he travelled first north to Boscobel, then south via the Cotswolds and the Mendips to the South Coast, and finally along the South Downs to Shoreham where he escaped to France.

Accompanied by a deep ditch just inside the boundary on your left, walk to the bottom of the first field where you cross a stile on the left and then resume your former heading, now with the ditch and hedge at your right hand. (You may recognise this path – it was partly covered, in the opposite direction, on Walk 19 in *Country Walks*.) Stay with the hedge-and-ditch and, about 300 yards after a brief gravel-surfaced section, change to walk on its right-hand side.

Very soon, on the edge of a bramble patch, you may notice the tall, spiny heads of teasel. These heads were, in times past, used for separating out the fibres of wool prior to spinning and even for raising the pile on the baize on snooker tables!

As you approach houses, the path curves to the right to reach a road into which you turn left and walk into the village of Little Alne, passing an antiques and craft centre as you go. When you reach a road junction (sign-posted Aston Cantlow and Bearley), turn right. You soon reach a bridge over the River Alne, noticing the many ancient, pollarded willows which surround it. Continue on the road and, about 150 yards beyond the bridge (and just before the turn-off for Aston Cantlow), take a left turn and cross a stile leading to a long-abandoned railway route.

In about 150 yards, the track divides. Here, you go left and, in about 50 yards, cross a stile on the right and join a well-trodden path across the field ahead of you, which may be marshy in places. Cross a metal footbridge and the stile beyond it and then bear very slightly right to a gateway at the other side of the field, negotiating a ditch halfway across. Now walk on with an intermittent hawthorn hedge, occasionally reinforced by barbed wire, at your right hand.

The boundary becomes even more dilapidated and, as you near a three-arched railway bridge, you pass between gateposts to walk to a stile in front of the bridge. Cross the stile, walk under the railway bridge, turn left over a green-railed road bridge and, just before the road swings under the railway, take a footpath which runs along the base of the railway embankment and with a ditch and a concrete roadway on the right. At the end of this path, cross a stile and the concrete-surfaced road beyond it and, aiming for the right hand corner of the security fencing of a water-treatment unit, walk across the field.

As you crossed the last stile, you may have noticed what appeared to be an ivy tree on the opposite side of the concrete road. In fact, what you saw was a hawthorn tree (or was it four?) festooned with ivy which, being only a climber, had used the hawthorn(s) as its supporting scaffold.

When you reach the river, notice how its meanderings have eroded its banks. Pass through a wicket gate between the fence and the river and walk beside the Alne on a path which can be very muddy. At the end of the fence, cross a stile and, bearing slightly right, cross a stream via a short concrete causeway and then pass through a gateway to continue with the river on your right.

When you reach the second bridge (this a metal footbridge), swing left up a short grassy incline and walk ahead on a ridge leading in the direction of the squat tower of Wootton Wawen church. Ahead on your right is the splendid Wootton Hall, built in 1687. Via a wooden kissing gate and then a stout five-barred gate, you reach the busy Birmingham-Stratford road (A3400). Carefully cross this – there is a handily-placed pedestrian refuge on you left – and walk up a short lane to the church.

Do try to make time to look inside St Peter's Church which is said to be the oldest church in Warwickshire, parts of it dating back to the eighth century. Its informative guide book will enhance your visit.

Having visited the church, retrace your steps to the main road, cross it and turn right to walk past interesting houses pausing as you get past Dial House to notice, on its western gable, a sundial above which are the words *Veritas temporis pater* – 'Truth, the Father of Time'. At the road junction, bear left onto Alcester Road (B4089) to reach the end of the walk.

If you have travelled by train, continue up Alcester Road, go straight ahead on Wawensmere Road to the station.

16
Three Picturesque
Mid-Worcestershire Villages

This gentle walk, through Crowle, Huddington and Himbleton, explores pleasant countryside and visits Huddington Court and some fine churches.

Start: Crowle, Old Chequers Inn (GR 920565).
Distance: 8½ miles; shorter option 6½ miles.
Maps: Landranger 150; Pathfinder 996.
Parking: There may be sufficient space on the side of the short lane leading from the main road to the Old Chequers Inn; otherwise roadsides in Netherwood Lane.
Public transport: Buses 352/353 running between Worcester and Droitwich provide a limited service to Crowle. Leave the bus at Crowle Garage and walk back to the Old Chequers Inn.
Refreshments: The Old Chequers Inn (Crowle) and the Galton Arms (Himbleton).

THE walk starts at the west end of the main road through Crowle at the road junction to the Old Chequers Inn and Netherwood Lane (GR920565). To the extreme left (east) of the inn car park, you will locate an enclosed green path leading away from you. Join this and walk ahead to pass through a kissing gate. Then, with a field boundary on your left, continue to the next kissing gate beyond which you go straight ahead towards the church.

At the far corner of a red-brick wall, turn left through a wicket gate and, in 50 yards, pass through a kissing gate on your right. Continue ahead with the boundary at your left hand until another kissing gate and a flight of steps leads you down to an asphalt path across the graveyard of St John the Baptist Church.

This is the first of four churches which may be visited on this walk, all of them, at the time of writing, still left open on weekdays. Of note in this one is a richly carved rood screen and a twelfth century lectern of smooth grey limestone which lay neglected in the churchyard for many years until it was re-installed, on a new marble-pillared pedestal, in 1841.

Leaving the church through its fourteenth century porch, walk back across the graveyard to the steps but, instead of going up them, turn half right and walk down a lane to a road. Here turn left and, in a further 50 yards, take a right turn (indicted by a signpost) through a gate marked Pinners Close and, in 20 yards or so, go ahead on an enclosed (and sometimes muddy) path on the left, initially overhung by tall *Cupressus leylandii*. On reaching a cross-track immediately before new buildings, turn left and walk on to join a road (Froxmere Road) into which you turn right.

73

When the main housing ends and the road narrows, walk up a signposted drive just past house no. 71 on your left. Very soon cross a stile and continue ahead beneath mistletoe-laden apple trees to turn right through a wooden wicket gate just before an attractive garden. Walk straight down the next meadow to cross a stile at its bottom left-hand corner to emerge onto a lane. Turn left and in a further 60 yards or so, opposite an old timber-framed barn, go through a gate on your right into a large field in which is an old wind-pump.

Walk forward to cross a stile in a wire fence which now divides what was originally a single field. Your next stile is in the far left-hand corner of this next field in front of a long, red brick barn. Cross this stile and walk on with the hedge on your right. When the hedge begins to veer off to the right, continue with it for a few yards and then proceed across the field aiming for a stile some 40 yards from its far right-hand corner. As you go, you may be serenaded, in springtime, by a rooks' chorus.

Cross this stile and, with care, the wooden footbridge beyond it and then bear right to follow the margin of the field, initially along the banks of Bow Brook and later beside a spinney. At the end of the spinney, climb over a stile and immediately turn right to cross a stile and sleeper bridge which are in

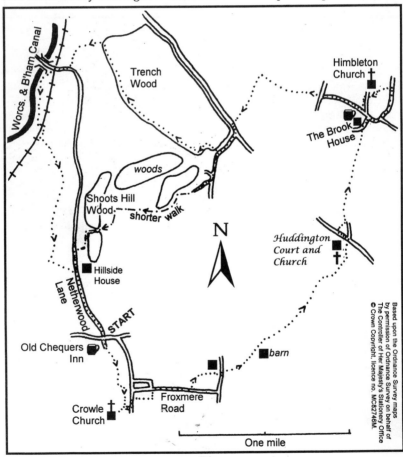

the shadow of the trunk of a grotesquely-shaped dead oak. Having done this, turn left and continue through two fields, the second much longer than the first, as you head towards Huddington, now with the hedge at your left hand.

At the end of the second field, do not go through the gate ahead but bear right and, in about 80 yards, cross the brook by way of a footbridge. Walk across a large paddock, aiming for the black-and-white church tower. On coming within 20 yards of farm buildings, enter a farm yard via a stile on your right and, in about 30 yards, bear left to walk between a barn built of grey breeze-blocks and, on your left, another of old, red brick.

You now find yourself on a concrete drive which leads you through a farm gate and then through wrought iron gates. Now prepare yourself for a spectacular sight for, in 4 or 5 yards, when you turn left between clipped yews, you are confronted with Huddington Court. Immediately beyond the yews, turn left to cross a lawn to reach the church. (There is private access only to Huddington Court itself.)

Huddington Court

Take time, as you cross the lawn, to admire the moated Huddington Court of which Vivian Bird writes: 'There is no more charming house in Britain' with 'its breathtaking black and white glories... a jewel perfectly set among smooth lawns and colourful gardens'. Seeing is believing!

Having visited the church and having seen, in its graveyard, a memorial to an unknown man, thought to be a soldier escaping from the Battle of Worcester in the 1651, go back across the lawn and, having passed between the yews, turn left to continue down the drive to a road. Here turn left and, in a little over a hundred yards, you come to a double footpath sign. If you wish to see more of Huddington Court, take the path of your left and walk on for about 150 yards to a black-and-white cottage. From here, retrace your steps to the road and cross the stile on the other side.

Your path now crosses the field and you should aim for the stile just to the left of the pair of pretty black-and-white cottages. Cross the lawns in front of these cottages and, when you reach the right-hand corner of them, bear slightly left to cross a stile which leads you through a spinney. Having soon emerged from this, continue with the field margin on your right. At the end of the field, two stiles and a plank bridge lead you to a clear path across the next field at the far side of which a footbridge and, in 20 yards, a further stile lead you to another clearly-defined path which takes you towards Himbleton. Walkers are grateful to farmers like the one on whose land you are now walking for observing the regulations by reinstating footpaths after cultivation.

Cross a stile at the end of this field and continue slightly left between a row of young conifers and Shell Brook on your right. During floods in April 1998, the wettest April of the century, this path was several feet deep in water. On reaching a lane, turn right, noticing on your left another fine black-and-white property, The Brook House, and, high above you on the right, abundant mistletoe again. At the T-junction, turn right and walk on for about 100 yards, crossing a bridge *en route*.

At a road junction, turn left (signed Shell, Bradley Green and Feckenham) and walk along this lane for about a quarter of a mile when you turn left onto a path and, by way of two footbridges, soon reach the church of St Mary Magdalene, Himbleton with its timbered, shingle-roofed tower.

What may have been a piece of remarkable social engineering is to be seen in this barrel-roofed church. On the south side of the nave is the Shell Chapel, built on in the fourteenth century to accommodate worshippers from Shell, a hamlet not a mile north of Himbleton but, for some reason, in need of segregation.

Leave the churchyard via the richly-carved lych gate at its west end and turn left to follow a narrow lane as it soon swings off to the right to a T-junction where you turn left. Continue ahead until you reach a main road where, as you face the gates of The Brook House, you turn right. Walk on past the public house for a further quarter-mile until you reach another T-junction where you cross the road and go straight ahead onto a green lane.

In springtime, you may come across the elegant yellow flowers of cowslips which are frequent hereabouts. This plant was, according to some records, once almost as common as the buttercup in our countryside. Though over-picking of its flowers for decoration and wine-making may have had some effect, modern agricultural methods, such as replacement of old meadows by 'improved grassland' and the widespread use of herbicides, must be the major cause of the decline of this delightful plant.

Continue on the green lane (which, after it narrows, can become difficult after very wet weather) for about half a mile, as you go crossing a stile, passing a fallen tree and walking between arches of blackthorn. The lane ends in a circular patch of rough grass where a farm gate faces you. Here, on your right you will see a waymarked stile. Do not cross this but, with your back to it, go slightly left across the field ahead of you to a waymarked wooden footbridge. At the other side of this, go half left across the next field, aiming midway between a red brick, double-gabled house and a black and white farmhouse in the distance. Cross a stile and walk ahead, with the hedge on your left, to come to a road onto which you turn left. Reaching a road junction after 100 yards, turn right (signed Sale Green and Crowle) and walk ahead.

On your right is Trench Wood and in 160 yards, just before the Sale Green village sign, you reach a gate on your right which gives access to a Nature Reserve run jointly by the Worcestershire Nature Conservation Trust and the British Butterfly Conservation Society. Trench Wood is famed for nightingales though recently numbers have been in decline.

Leaving the Nature Reserve gate behind, continue on the road for a little over 100 yards where the two routes separate. For the **longer** route now continue reading from ★ below.

Following the **shorter** route continue on the road through Sale Green and turn into the second lane on your right (unfortunately nameless – but it is opposite a wooden roadside seat). The surface soon deteriorates as the lane swings to the left. At the end of the lane, near the last house, look out for a stile on your left (which may easily be overlooked). Having crossed this, turn right and continue ahead with woodland edge on your right, enjoying good views over Worcestershire, with Bredon Hill possibly visible in the far south.

About 130 yards past the next stile, just after the woodland ends, you reach a stile and plank bridge in the thick hedge on your right. Negotiate these and then turn left and walk up the left-hand edge of a long field. At the top of the incline, pass through a gate and turn left onto a muddy lane. After about 100 yards, climb over a stile on your right and cross the field and the stile at its opposite side. Your path then slopes down through scrubby woodland, the smell of wild garlic being noticeable in springtime.

After crossing another stile, the path continues downwards, now hugging the edge of Shoots Hill Wood on your left which, in their season, is spectacularly carpeted with bluebells. Follow the margin of the wood as it curves left and, at the end of the field, walk to the right soon to reach a lane (Netherwood Lane) onto which you turn left. Walk on and, just under 100 yards after passing the gates of Hillside House, you rejoin the longer route at ✪ on page 78.

★ Following the **longer** route turn right onto a green lane immediately after a bungalow called Little Half Acre. The green lane soon gives way to a meandering, muddy path on which you stay, ignoring side branches, until you reach a crosspath where you are confronted with a 'Private – Keep Out' notice. Here, turn left and when the path forks, in just under 100 yards, take the right-hand option enjoying the sweet smell of bluebells in their flowering season.

Bluebells thrive in many woods in the Midlands. However, in parts of the country, bluebell woods have been devastated by the large-scale extraction of bulbs for sale to gardeners – despite the heavy penalties available under the 1981 Wildlife and Countryside Act.

When you reach the edge of the wood, swing right and continue on a path just inside the wood's margin (don't take the path that will lead you back into the wood), the dog-tooth-shaped Malvern ridge being visible, on clear days, to your left. As you pass through the woodland, you may be lucky enough to see a muntjac deer dashing away into cover ahead of you. At the end of the thick woodland, pass through a gate and continue on the edge of the ridge through wooded grazing land where primroses are abundant in spring.

When this gives way to an open field, turn sharply left and walk down the slope, aiming a little to the left of Oddingly church tower, to cross a stile at the bottom. Continue ahead with the hedge on your left until some 20 yards after turning right at the field's corner you reach and pass through a gate. Cross a stream and then turn left, aiming for a stile by a gate on the far left-hand margin of the field. Cross this stile to reach a lane onto which you turn right and soon, very cautiously, walk over a level-crossing.

If you wish to take a half-mile diversion to visit Oddingly church, continue over the canal bridge and follow the lane as it swings right and then left. You soon see a signpost to the church which is reached down an avenue of lime trees.

Missing out the diversion, take a path down to the right about 15 yards beyond a level-crossing. This leads to the towpath of the reed-fringed Worcester and Birmingham Canal. Turn left under the bridge and walk on for about a quarter of a mile until the towpath runs close to the railway line. Just as it veers away again, look out for a stile on the left (of course!) which is just beyond a narrow wedge of grassland surrounded by barbed wire. Cross this and its neighbour and then, *with great care*, the railway track beyond. Go down the stony staircase on the other side and cross the awkward stile at the bottom.

Now turn right and walk along the edge of the field for 150 yards or so when you will see, above you at the top of the railway embankment, a signal (though this may be partly obscured by trees). Here turn sharply left and cross a stile partly-hidden in the hedge opposite. Having done this, turn right and follow the field margin for 75 yards where you cross stiles and a plank bridge on your right.

After this, go half left to cross another footbridge and then half right across the next field to a double stile above which you can see the white gable-end of a house. Beyond this, go straight across the next, tapering field until, in its far corner, you cross another double stile to enter a narrow strip of grassland. Go ahead on this, with a brook at your right-hand side.

The strip gradually widens out and about 150 yards after the second of two further stiles, ignoring a footbridge on the right, go left over a plank bridge and walk ahead, passing to the right of isolated hawthorn bushes, to reach and cross a stile. Now continue ahead up a wire-enclosed path to reach a lane (Netherwood Lane). Here you turn right and are joined by those who have walked the shorter route.

◐ From here, you continue on Netherwood Lane for a little over a quarter of a mile, getting occasional glimpses of the Malverns through gaps in the hedge on the right, to your starting point in Crowle, using the strategically-placed mirror to help you to cross safely to the Old Chequers Inn.

17
A Walk around 'Ambridge'

This walk starts and finishes in Inkberrow which is the model of Ambridge, the Archers' BBC village. It goes through an attractive bluebell wood and also visits two other delightful Worcestershire villages, one with a most interesting village green.

Start: Inkberrow village green (GR015573)
Distance: 8½ miles, shorter option 6 miles.
Maps: Landranger 150; Pathfinder 997.
Parking: Roadsides on the road leading from the village green towards the church, Inkberrow.
Public Transport: Buses 350 (Redditch-Worcester) and 71 (Bromsgrove-Stratford) stop at The Bull's Head, near the village green.
Refreshments: The Bull's Head and The Old Bull in Inkberrow.

L EAVING the village green, walk east, down past the Old Bull, the model for The Bull in 'The Archers' radio series. In the Ambridge Bar of this 500 year old pub you will find photos of some of the cast. Close to these a glass panel reveals some of the original wattle and daub which still forms part of the building's walls. St Peter's church on your right is entered via a lych gate which is a memorial to those thirty-one men who died in World War I and three who died in the 1939-45 conflict.

Having had your eyes raised to look at its battlements and the weird gargoyles, beware, if you enter the church, of the steps immediately inside the main door.

The Old Bull, Inkberrow

Opposite the church is the rectory where Charles I stayed overnight on his journey to Naseby, leaving behind him maps which are still in existence. From the lych gate, rejoin the road, turn right and walk down a sunken lane, initially under the boughs of a very large cedar tree. At the bottom of the lane, turn right at a T-junction and, in about 15 yards, take a track off to the left (signed Cladswell and Cookhill). Follow this track until you reach and cross a stile beside a farm gate. Facing you is a sharp incline. Go up this, aiming 10 yards to the right of an ash tree on the horizon, this tree having

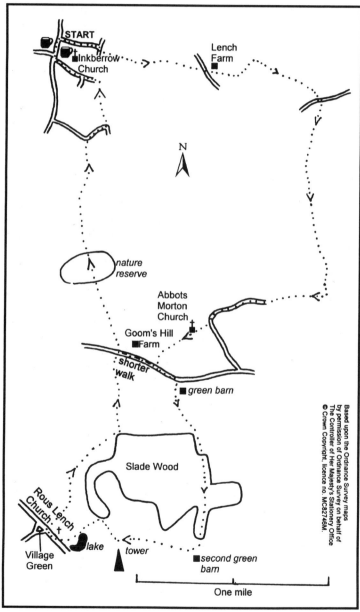

80

curious, bulbous swellings at the base of its trunk.

At the top, pass through a gap to the right of another old ash and proceed across the field to a stile about 100 yards ahead of you. Cross this stile and, veering slightly *right*, walk to a another one on the other side of the field, about 70 yards away. When you have climbed over this one, walk half-left up a slope to reach and cross another stile which is beside an overgrown sandpit (ignoring a nearby path going off to the left). Your next objective is a little to the right of a house across and down the field, this house being red-bricked with its nearer gable-end painted white (Lench Farm).

Cross a stile here and go half-right across the lane to cross another. Walk across the field ahead of you aiming immediately to the right of the nearer electricity post, pass through a gap in the hedge and, veering very slightly right, soon reach and cross a stile about 20 yards to the right of the right-hand corner of the field. Here, turn left onto a bridleway. This is initially enclosed but, 120 yards after its left-hand hedge is lost, turn right through a wide gap by an old oak.

Just before this oak, amongst the plants growing in the hedge bottom on your right, you will in summer be aware of the bright yellow flowers of St John's Wort. This plant is now achieving commercial importance as a substitute for a widely used antidepressant drug.

Having turned right by the oak, cut across the field, a quarter-left aiming for a wooden footbridge lying at the right-hand end of a patch of woodland. Beyond the bridge, walk on with the woodland initially close at your left hand and then going ahead to cross a stile just beyond an electricity post. Passing a track on the left continue up a wide track for about 120 yards where you cross a stile on your left and follow a rough, enclosed path which passes behind houses to reach a lane. (In summer, this path can become totally impassable due to rampant nettles and briars. The track which you have just left leads up to the lane and walkers have been known to use it when the footpath is blocked.) On reaching the lane, turn left.

After about 25 yards (or a little further if the footpath was impassable) turn right onto a rough lane which, in 70 yards, swings to the left. At this point, you go straight ahead through a gate and walk on with the boundary on your left, this containing some grotesquely-shaped oaks. 200 yards into the second field, stay on the same heading as you pass to the left of a pool, through a thicket. (If the vegetation blocks your progress here you may find it necessary to detour to the right of the pool, soon to rejoin the path by the hedge.

At the end of this field, proceed through a wicket gate, walk on for 10 yards and then turn *left* onto an enclosed bridleway which can, as is usual with bridleways, be very muddy at times. Stay on this path for nearly 300 yards and, as you reach the end of the field on your right, look out carefully for a stile close to an old oak with a Y-shaped trunk. Cross this stile and go ahead with the field boundary at your right hand.

When the hedge swings abruptly to the right, carry on straight across the field aiming for a hedge-gap opposite. Walk on, now following a tractor track, until you enter a field with paddock railings on your left. Continue ahead and soon follow the railings as they swing left, now enabling you to walk on a firmer-surfaced farm track. After 100 yards or so, continue straight ahead as the track veers off to the right towards a corrugated iron barn. Soon cross a stile over wooden palings and walk on to reach a road.

You are now in the quiet village of Abbots Morton. (*For an interesting diversion, turn left and walk for about 100 yards down the road. You will notice, on your left, Mulberry House complete with, in its front garden, a mulberry tree, a species thought to have been introduced to Britain by the Romans. Then retrace your steps back along the road.*) If you haven't followed this diversion, turn right and walk on to the end of the main street. Having admired the various styles of old houses. Bear slightly right, up stone steps, to enter the churchyard soon to pass, on your left, a modest, moss-covered stone commemorating the Silver Jubilee of King George V in 1935.

The charm of the tiny church of St Peter is in its peaceful simplicity. Amongst other interesting features inside is a display of ancient bell-clappers, the oldest of which dates from 1410, and a coloured photograph of Miss Margaret Roberts, who had been the church's faithful organist for 60 years.

Leave the churchyard by way of a kissing gate at its far (west) end and walk along the left-hand margins of the next two fields (though with a hedge having been removed these may become merged into one). At the end of the second field go through a waymarked kissing gate and continue with a hedge on the left. Cross a stile beside a gate and pass houses (one of which started life as a National School building in 1845) and farm buildings to reach a road via a drive and a gate.

Here, the **shorter** *route diverges. If you are following this, turn right and walk along the road for about 300 yards where, just beyond Goom's Hill Farm, you rejoin the main route on page 83 at ★.*

For the **longer** route, turn left and walk for 250 yards when, just before reaching the back of a 'road bends' sign, you turn off to the right onto a track. Walking to the right of a large, green barn, you follow a firm tractor track for a further 250 yards or so where, just as you leave woodland on your right and the track bends right, you bear left through a farm gate and aim for the left-hand corner of woodland ahead (Slade Wood). Reaching this, walk on with the wood on your right, soon crossing three stiles in quick succession, the third one leading into this bluebell wood on a path which (initially and later) runs close to its eastern margin. You will, in spring and early summer, enjoy abundant birdsong here.

150 yards after leaving the wood via a wicket gate, you reach another green barn. (In this barn, the writer once encountered an albino pheasant and pondered on the limited chances of survival afforded by its unfortunate mutation!) Immediately *before* the barn, turn right and walk up an incline between newly planted trees.

About 150 yards beyond a gate at the top, cross a stile close to the hedge on your left and then proceed slightly right to another under a mistletoe-bearing lime tree which is near the southern tip of Slade Wood. Having gone over this stile, look across to a line of straggly pine trees at the other side of the field (not to be confused with the large ones surrounding the red-brick tower on your left). Your next stile is about a quarter of the way along the row of pines, measuring from the left.

The tower is in the grounds of The Court which is famed for its yew hedges. It was, according to Vivian Bird, built in the late 1800s to relieve unemployment during a hard winter.

There may be confusing waymarks on this stile, but walk straight ahead down an incline, passing a waymark post and in the direction of a white house, the top of which may be visible half-a-mile ahead, amongst trees. From this vantage point you may, on clear days, have good views from the Clees and Abberley Hills on the right to the Malverns on the left. Cross two more stiles to enter parkland and walk on, passing just to the right of a wire fence which separates you from a newly-created ornamental lake.

When this fence veers left continue *slightly* left to reach, in 300 yards or so, fencing adjacent to woodland behind which is the moat of the original Manor. Walk on, soon to enter the graveyard of Rous Lench's St Peter's Church (the third dedication of that name on today's walk) by a metal kissing gate and a short avenue of yews. This is another gem, with Norman doors, interesting gargoyles and pretty hellebores outside its south door. Continue past the south door in the same direction, passing the stump of an old yew tree which still bears surprising numbers of flourishing branches. In the far corner of the graveyard, old stone steps lead you onto a road (close to a bus shelter) where you turn right.

It is worth spending a few minutes on the delightful village green which lies a few yards down the road to your right. An oak, planted on Jubilee Day in 1935, gives you an idea of the growth rate of such trees. You will also see the elaborately-tiled structure housing a post box, the tastefully-modernised Old School House (1864) complete with bell tower, a well beneath a shingled cover and a splendid yew arch. A seat commemorating the Jubilee of Queen Elizabeth II in 1977 will provide a pleasant resting spot.

Your exit from the village green lies 40 yards from the bus shelter. Cross a stile and walk up the driveway to the left of the cream-coloured Park Cottage and then pass to the left of a small barn (which houses an old cider press) and continue through a paddock which you leave by way of a stile by a green-painted shed. Now walk ahead, aiming for your next gate which is in line with the left-hand edge of the woodland ahead (Slade Wood) above which you may see buzzards effortlessly soaring.

Go ahead across the next field on a faint, tractor track, the village ahead in the distance being Inkberrow and the conspicuous red tower to its left being, incredibly, a transmitter station of a mobile phone company. At the end of the field, go through a gate and go slightly right onto a grassy bridleway along which you continue, with the hedge on your right. At the end of the second field, pass through a metal gate, turn left and, with a hedge on your left, walk through three fields to a road. Here, turn right, cross the road and, in 50 yards, immediately before Goom's Hill Farm, cross a stile on your left.

★ *The shorter route rejoins here.*

Walk ahead through an extended farmyard, the hedge on your left, until a second stile leads you into a field. Continue straight ahead until, in the far left-hand corner, you cross a pair of stiles and an unsteady plank bridge. Continue across the next field, on the same heading, to cross a footbridge over Piddle Brook.

You have now entered Long Meadow Nature Reserve. The reserve is a permanent, lowland water meadow and is owned and managed by the Worcestershire Wildlife Trust and contains some unusual plants and a colony of badgers. (Beware of holes in the path which, in summer, can be concealed by the lush vegetation.)

From the bridge, walk straight up the slope ahead, passing the badger setts near the top. Leave the Reserve via a stile (with a badger gate beside it) and continue on a path which soon runs beside a hedge. Walk on, with the hedge on your right and, at the end of the field, go through hawthorn trees to cross a stile and continue on your former heading on a well-trodden path across the next field.

Passing to the right of a low, twin-trunked oak, go through a gap in the hedge, bear left and follow the field margin until the hedge goes off abruptly to your left. Continue ahead, slightly left, to cross a stile and walk on with a hedge now on your right. Your path follows this hedge until, as it begins to slope down more steeply, the path cuts diagonally left across the field in the direction of Inkberrow church tower. (If the path is obstructed by crops it may be necessary to carry on round the field margin, bearing left at the bottom of the incline.)

In the bottom left-hand corner of the field, you climb over a multi-barred stile at the base of an ash tree. Now continue, with a brook on your right, until, by way of another stile, you reach a lane onto which you turn right. Continue along the lane until, just before an attractive thatched cottage, you bear left onto a bridleway (signed Crabtree Lane). In about 20 yards, cross a stile on your left.

You are faced with two stiles. Ignore them both but aim for the corner of the fence which is just to the right of them. Now walk on through a paddock with the fence, topped with barbed wire, on your left. This paddock gradually narrows and, just beyond a pool at its far end, you cross a stile and enter a patch of woodland through which a clear track leads up a gradual slope. Follow this path which soon veers abruptly left and leads down to a footbridge. Beyond this, walk straight ahead beside a *Cupressus leylandii* hedge.

Plants of this species have attracted much publicity in recent years owing to their prolific rate of growth - three feet or more per year. Although obviously not the case here, they have led to expensive disputes between neighbours when planted close to boundaries, featuring in television programmes where they have been described as 'horticultural vandals' and other less-flattering names. Mr C.J.Leyland clearly didn't appreciate the trouble he would cause when he propagated this hybrid late in the 1800s!

At the end of the hedge, cross a stile on your left, and walk ahead on a gravel path in front of Rock End Cottage soon to veer right to walk up a lane, noticing an unusual bird-refuge made from an old barrel. When the lane reaches a road (Pepper Street), go straight ahead and follow it up to the main road (A422). Here, turn right and walk onwards to the village green where you began your journey.

When you reach the village green again, you may wish to pause on the circular seat commemorating Queen Elizabeth II's Silver Jubilee and, if your walk has been at Christmastide, take advantage of the mistletoe above your head.

18

Villages, Dolls and Teddy Bears

Several small, quiet Warwickshire villages are visited on this walk, stunning views can unfold and there is an opportunity to visit a pub with an unusual toy collection.

Start: Evesham-Stratford road east of Alcester. (GR122565).
Distance: 7½ miles (7 miles without diversion to the Golden Cross).
Maps: Landranger 150; Pathfinder 997.
Parking: In lay-by near Toll Bar Cottage on the A46 Evesham-Stratford road east of Alcester.
Public Transport: 146 MRW service to Wixford (*adds 1½ miles*). Leave the bus at the Three Horseshoes pub in Wixford and take the road opposite, signed Exhall Village ¾. Then at the fork go left and walk about three quarters of a mile into Wixford. Entering the village look out on the right for a post box by Glebe Farm, then start reading from ★ on page 87.
Refreshments: The Golden Cross, Ardens Grafton. *For bus passengers*, The Three Horseshoes, Wixford.
Places of interest: The Vardy-Smith Collection of dolls and teddy bears at the Golden Cross. *For opening times phone 01789 772420.*

USING the grass verge, walk on *carefully* from the lay-by in the direction of Stratford for about 150 yards. Cross the stile on the left and then proceed with the field boundaries on your left. At the end of the second field, pass through a gate by a gnarled and hollow ash tree and then walk on for about 80 yards where you go left through another gate. Continue, now with an intermittent hedge on your right.

Soon after passing a barn with a rusty corrugated-iron roof, go through the gateway ahead and walk along a muddy lane and through the farmyard of Manor Farm to reach a road. Here, you turn right into Orchard Corner at the end of which cul-de-sac you turn left onto a bridleway (blue markers) on which you stay as it winds its way up to the church. The bridleway passes along in front of the church, the graveyard of which is entered at its east end after passing through a farm gate on the left and then a wood and metal kissing gate.

The Church of St Mary and All Saints occupies a commanding position overlooking the village of Haselor. Hiding behind a yew tree in the north-west corner of its graveyard lies an unusual tombstone. An old millstone commemorates Albert Crampton Stewart and his wife Katharine of Hoo Mill (which lies on the River Alne about a mile to the west).

A cobweb of paths radiates from here so ensure that you select the correct one – you need the tarmacked path that leads down from the metal kissing gate at the west end of the church towards the village. On reaching a road, turn left and follow it as it swings right by Manor Farm (past which you walked earlier). About 150 yards from this sharp bend, the road veers off to the left. Here you walk straight ahead on a tractor track.

150 yards into the second field, go through a gateway on your right and continue on the same heading with the boundary now on your left. Walk on down this field and pass through a gate and in about 50 yards, pass though another gate, on your left, and continue with the hedge now on your right. When you reach the next gate on your right, pass through it and then walk on, with the hedge on your left, to reach a road by way of a stile and plank bridge.

Turn left and walk on for about 40 yards where you divert onto a lane on your right. This takes you past a water company depot and under the A46.

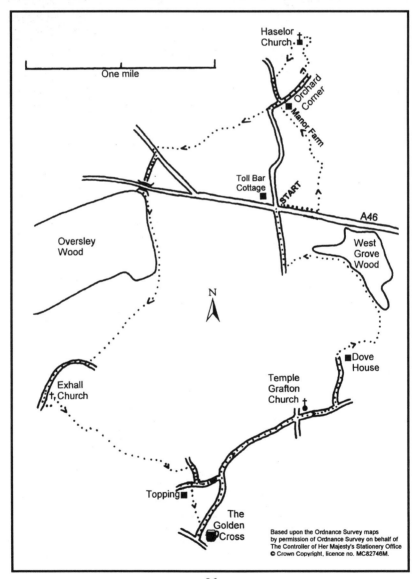

Based upon the Ordnance Survey maps by permission of Ordnance Survey on behalf of The Controller of Her Majesty's Stationery Office © Crown Copyright, licence no. MC82746M.

Haselor Church

On the other side of the underpass, bear slightly left and then right onto a tractor track which initially runs alongside Oversley Wood. On passing through the first gateway veer very slightly right and then continue on your original heading, now with newly-planted trees at your right hand.

Go through the next gate, a metal wicket type, and walk ahead with a ditch and hedge on your left, serenaded in spring by bleating lambs. In the distance ahead of you, on clear days you may see Bredon Hill and Broadway Tower. After about 400 yards, pass through a gate straight ahead of you and continue, now with ditch and hedge on your right. Soon after walking past Valley Farm, you reach a road onto which you turn right and walk into Exhall village, the verdigris-covered tower of the church coming into view as you do so.

Bus travellers now continue along the road to return to Wixford.

Immediately past the church, you see a post box in the wall.

★ *Bus travellers start here.*

Beside the post box walk up an incline into the churchyard.

This church is dedicated to St Giles, a hermit who, in the ninth century, is reputed to have lived near Arles in southern France and to have owned a pet deer. A king, out hunting, fired an arrow at the hind which was hiding in some undergrowth. Riding into the thicket to collect his victim, the King found Giles, himself injured by the arrow, with the hind protected in his arms. Hence, maybe, the fact that St Giles' emblem is the arrow – though no such emblem is to be found in the church. On the north side and only visible from the outside, is a doorway, complete with studded door, which is a remnant of the original twelfth century building.

Leaving the church by its modern porch, turn left and walk along an asphalt path to pass through a metal wicket gate. Turn right and, with barns initially on your right, walk along a cart track. After the barns, you continue with the hedge on you right for just over half a mile. Cross a stile, then a stream by way of a rough, concrete bridge, then another stile. As you approach the houses of Ardens Grafton sitting on the horizon, cross an

87

easily-missed double stile plus wooden bridge on your right and then continue for about 50 yards or so on your original bearing, with the hedge now on your left.

After crossing the next stile turn three-quarters right and walk up a slope to another stile. Having crossed this, walk three-quarters left, continuing to walk up across the slope. The stile you are aiming for, less prominent than the previous two, is adjacent to the uppermost of two large sheds. Having negotiated this stile, walk to the right of a cottage's greenhouse, soon to reach a road onto which you turn right. Walk up a sharp incline, at the top of which you have a choice.

If you do not wish to visit the Golden Cross, turn left and walk about 200 yards. When you reach a major road junction, rejoin the main route at ✪ .

To reach the Golden Cross, turn right and walk along a lane for about 50 yards. When you reach a house called 'Topping', turn left onto its drive and walk towards and through an ornamental metal gate to the left of the house. Continue through its rear garden, passing a metal anchor on your way and enjoying, on clear days, a fabulous panorama stretching from the Malverns well to the east of Broadway Tower. Leave the garden by a stile and follow the hedge down to a road. Here turn right and, in about 150 yards you reach the pub with its unique collection of toys.

The Vardy-Smith Collection of dolls and teddy bears is extensive. The inmates range from three inches to three feet in height and are of German, French and English origin, some dating from the 1850s. A wide range of refreshments is also available. Opening times may be checked by telephoning 01789 772420.

Leaving the Golden Cross, retrace your steps and walk up the road into Ardens Grafton. When you reach a T-junction in about 600 yards, turn right.

✪ *Join here if you didn't divert to the Golden Cross.*

Walk along the pavement for half-a-mile or so to the adjacent village of Temple Grafton. Continue ahead at the crossroads, soon to reach the church of St Andrew with its timbered belfry and shingled spire.

The original church, dating from Saxon times, was rebuilt in 1875. Inside, there is a tablet in memory of Thomas King who, in 1877, bequeathed £180 which must have been, in that time, a substantial sum. The money was to be invested in 'King's Charity', 'the interest to be distributed annually in January by the Vicar and Churchwardens to the deserving poor resident in the Parish of Grafton'.

As with the church at Binton (visited on Walk 19), as you stand in the porch, you will hear (if it has been wound up) the church clock ticking away above your head. Walk back to the road and turn left. As the road begins to descend sharply, cross it to use the pavement on the far side, noticing, as you go down the slope, the statues of two Grecian ladies in a garden on the other side of the road.

At the bottom of the bank, cross the road and, just before a telephone kiosk, turn into a lane on the left. Walk past pollarded, ivy-clad willows and a noisy duck pond and, at the end of the lane, reach a house (Dove House). Continue straight ahead past the house and follow the hedge at your right hand as it goes forward and then curves to the right. You soon cross a plank bridge and continue, with the field boundary still on your right, until, in about 130 yards and soon after a prominent, solitary willow, you cross the line of a grubbed-out hedge. Here, turn left and proceed up a slope, soon walking on the right of a tall hedge and passing beneath triple electricity cables. At the top of the rise, go sharply left-right-right-left and continue ahead on your former bearing, with the hedge still at your left hand. In about 100 yards, cross a stile and then walk onwards along the curved edge of West Grove Wood.

This wood is planted predominantly with beeches in regular rows, primroses, bluebells and ground ivy all, in their season, colourfully decorating its floor.

At the wood's end, continue with a tall, neglected hedge on your left until you reach a road. Turn right onto this and walk down the incline until you see, ahead of you, Toll Bar Cottage where the walk began.

Bus travellers now continue reading from the start on page 85.

19

A Round Tour from Stratford-upon-Avon

A walk which starts in the 'tourist town' atmosphere but soon enters rural Warwickshire and visits some delightful villages.

Start: The Shakespeare Statue in Bancroft Gardens,
Stratford-upon-Avon.(GR205549)
Distance: 11½ miles; shorter option 3½ miles.
Parking: There are large car parks available in Stratford-upon-Avon.
Maps: Landranger 151; Pathfinder 997 & 998.
Public Transport: Stagecoach service X20 Birmingham/Stratford; BR to Stratford.
Refreshments: A large variety of establishments in Stratford; The Bell Inn and The Four Alls in Welford-on-Avon; The Bell in Shottery.

W ALK away from the statue with the Stratford Canal basin on your right. Swing left from the basin to pass to the right of Cox's Yard, formerly a timber merchant's premises and now housing a pub, a brewery, a Shakespeare exhibition and other visitor attractions. Cross the River Avon via the fine, old brick-arched footbridge, the Tramway Bridge, built in 1823 and which originally carried a horse-drawn tramway that connected the canal to Shipston-on-Stour and Moreton-in-Marsh. Look for the nature reserve island on your left as you cross the bridge.

At the far side of the bridge turn right into recreation grounds. Walk to the river and follow the riverside path, noticing the large numbers of swans, Canada geese and mallards soliciting food from visitors. After about half a mile, pass under a road bridge. Continue on the riverside path until, at the Colin P Winter lock, you turn left and walk up a twisting series of wooden steps, 55 in all.

The lock, built in 1971, was part of a five year scheme to restore the River Avon as a useable waterway. It had been made navigable in the seventeenth century but had steadily decayed and ceased to be used by commercial traffic in the middle of the last century. However, as the result of the efforts of dedicated volunteers, the Upper Avon was opened by the Queen Mother in 1974, an event commemorated by a modern monument beside the lock.

At the top of the steps continue your meandering walk down the Avon, which is now way down below you on your right. Proceed along the undulating path which gradually returns you to the level of the riverbank. When you reach the steel-girdered Stannels bridge, you veer left past brick arches and follow the field margin which runs parallel to the Greenway. Walk on until, soon after a kissing gate, you come to a smaller bridge, which allows the path to go beneath the Greenway. Here, the two routes diverge.

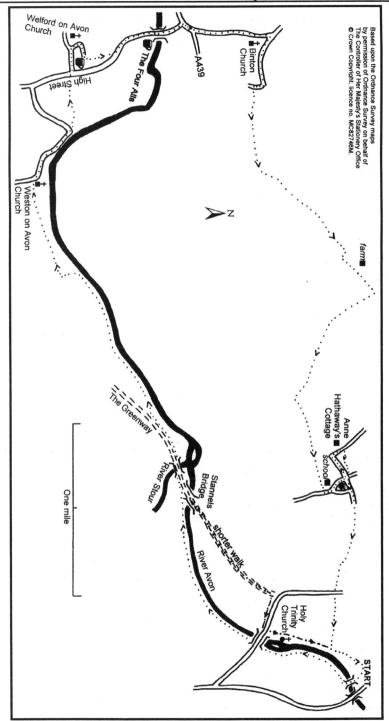

Based upon the Ordnance Survey maps
by permission of Ordnance Survey on behalf of
The Controller of Her Majesty's Stationery Office
© Crown Copyright, licence no. MC82746M.

Welford on Avon Church

Binton Church

A439

The Four Alls

High Street

N

farm

Weston on Avon Church

The Greenway

River Stour

One mile

Anne Hathaway's Cottage

School

Stannels Bridge

shorter walk

River Avon

Holy Trinity Church

START

The Greenway was, until 1976, the route of the Honeybourne Railway. This single line, originally built in 1859, was taken over by the Great Western Railway in 1906 and widened to a double track, the bridge which faces you showing its steel girders to have been cast in Chepstow in 1906 and used in that widening. The Greenway, five miles long, was opened in 1989 and is much-enjoyed by walkers, cyclists and horseriders.

For the shorter walk continue reading from the following paragraph. For the longer walk continue from ★ below.

Cross the stile just before the bridge and take a slanting path up to the Greenway. Continue on this, crossing the Avon and passing Stratford racecourse on your left. At a barrier just after the racecourse, two paths are directly ahead of you. Choose the left hand one of these and proceed to a car park where interesting information on the Greenway is displayed. After looking at the display, turn through 180^0 and walk across the car park to an asphalt path which leads, parallel to a busy road, down to the river. Turn left, go under the road bridge, past (*not* over) a footbridge and continue ahead on footpath and pavement to enter the churchyard of Holy Trinity Church.

In this beautiful church, William Shakespeare was baptised and his body, and those of Anne Hathaway and other members of his family, are buried. Do go in – but mind your head as you pass through its massive, panelled door!

Continue through the churchyard and, 35 yards beyond the gate at the far side, turn right into a park, pass a brass-rubbing centre and join a road (Waterside) along which you proceed past the Royal Shakespeare Theatre to your starting place.

★ Following the **longer** route use the bridge to pass under the Greenway. Having done this, turn left and, after crossing the River Stour via a footbridge, turn left again to resume your former heading with the Greenway on your left. At the field's end, make a ninety-degree turn to the right and walk to the Avon riverbank. Here turn left over a stile between a pair of ancient, pollarded willows and continue along the riverside for three-quarters of a mile.

Soon after passing the splendid row of poplars in front of Milcote Manor Farm (on the other side of the river is Luddington village), you reach the first building on the riverbank (brick-built and slate-roofed). 40 yards beyond this, the path swings left, away from the river. Follow this and, in about 75 yards, use a wooden footbridge to cross a stream.

The path soon leads back to the riverbank to pass a weir. Nearly 200 yards after this, follow the path as it veers away to the left again, this time up a slight incline. Ignoring a waymarked path in a few yards, continue on this path until, in about 100 yards, it reaches a bridleway. Turn right onto this unfenced track and stay on it as it becomes enclosed and passes horse paddocks as it approaches the village of Weston-on-Avon which, until 1931, would not have qualified for inclusion in this book as it was part of Gloucestershire.

The church of All Saints built in yellow stone which comes to life in sunlight has a squat, castellated tower and interesting gargoyles. The clear glass in the windows of the south side give glimpses of the church's neat interior.

Rejoin the bridleway and walk on for 40 yards to reach a lane into which you turn right. Walk ahead, admiring picturesque thatched cottages as you go. Continue to a crossroads where you take a bridleway to the right which runs parallel to a lane. This track gradually descends to reach the river again but, after about 200 yards, it leaves the river to ascend a slight slope beside a wooden fence and join a lane. In a further 30 yards, just beyond a house called Riverbank (and you need to look over your shoulder to see the name!), turn right to join a footpath.

When you come to a lane, turn right onto it and, in 20 yards, continue ahead on a clear path for just over a quarter of a mile, mainly across grass, finally to reach a busy road (High Street) in Welford-on-Avon. Cross the road to a small 'village green' with a seat for rest and the Bell Inn for refreshment. Behind the green, walk down Church Street past more delightful houses to St Peter's Church.

The first church on the site was built in 1059 but its only present-day remnant is the bowl of the font. In the early 1100s, a Norman church replaced its predecessor, the carved arch over the south door being one of its several features still in existence. The original lich gate (and that's the spelling preferred here) was built in the late 1300s but, because it had become unsafe, it was recently replaced with an exact replica.

Leaving the churchyard via the lich gate, turn left and immediately left again into Church Lane, a cul-de-sac. Follow this as it swings to the right by a magnificent horse-chestnut tree by the Rectory. Where the lane ends cross a stile on the left and follow a clear path with the wooded Binton Hill directly ahead of you. On reaching Binton Road, turn left and walk on for about 300 yards carefully crossing the road to reach the Four Alls public house.

Inside is an old painting, badly damaged by fire, beside which is an explanation of the name of the pub:

A king – I rule all,
A priest – I pray for all,
A soldier – I fight for all,
A yeoman – I pay for all.

... which reflects, perhaps, the grumbles of a tax-payer!

Just beyond the pub, the road narrows abruptly at Binton Bridges. To cross the first bridge, it is suggested that you wait for a gap in the traffic and walk in single file on the right hand side. Having reached the security of a pavement on the far side of the stone bridge, walk on to reach the A439 Stratford to Evesham road. You need to cross this busy road and it is best if you do so at this stage where you have optimum visibility. Some vehicles travel round the neighbouring bends at speed so please take great care!

Having reached the other side, turn right and, at the first junction, turn left and walk up the road to Binton, using the pavement on its far side. At the top of the hill, on the left, is a gurgling well, erected in 1868, with contradictory notices. Above is a stone tablet quoting a Biblical reference to thirst whilst below are (more-modern) additions warning you that the water is not fit for human consumption. Incidentally, the bowl of the well is surrounded by a luxuriant growth of liverworts, dark green, lowly plants which thrive in these damp, humid conditions. Having visited the well, carefully cross the road to Church Bank soon to reach St Peter's Church – and more gargoyles!.

Captain Robert Falcon Scott married Kathleen Bruce on September 2nd. 1908. Miss Bruce's brothers, Douglas and Lloyd Harvey, had been Rectors of Binton in the early 1900s. It is said that Capt. Scott and his wife spent their last weekend together in Binton before the explorer set off on his final, ill-fated expedition. The Scott memorial window and an interesting exhibition are to be seen at the west end of the church. As you leave, pause in the porch to enjoy the vista ahead over south Warwickshire whilst hearing the church clock ticking above you.

Leave the church porch, turn left and walk ahead between a pair of yew trees to a gate. Pass through this and walk on along the lane for nearly 400 yards where it swings to the right. 30 yards after the bend, you turn left onto a waymarked path. A stile leads to a paddock across which you walk, on the same bearing, to a stile just beyond a metal gate. Cross this and turn left to walk on an asphalt road to its T-junction where you turn right. In 30 yards, you reach a stile beyond which you turn left to proceed with the hedge on your left.

At the end of the hedge, having crossed one stile and passed one gap, look across the field to see a stile just to the right of a pair of oak trees. Turn right and walk round the field to this stile and cross it. Now, ignoring a waymark sign pointing directly ahead, turn three-quarters left and walk to a gateway in the far corner of the field. Standing in this gateway, on a low, stone bridge, you see your next stile directly ahead just over 200 yards across the field. As you cross the field note the old meanders of a stream, probably the Binton Brook that now runs to your right. On your left is some marked ridge and furrow.

Cross the stile and its twin and then proceed straight ahead with a wire fence at your left hand. At the end of this wire fence, cross a flat concrete bridge and the stile-cum-gate just beyond it. Now bear a quarter-left up the next field, aiming just to the right of farm buildings. At the top of the field, cross another stile and then go half-right for 50 yards to reach yet another one. Beyond this, turn left and continue with the hedge on your left. Immediately after the third stile, turn right, now continuing with the boundary on your right, soon ignoring a waymark inviting you to go left. Immediately after this, cross a stile and plank bridge which may be a little awkward to negotiate.

Continue up the gradual incline until, just less than 150 yards after passing a pair of robust, wooden electricity posts, the path swings left. Continue up the slope with the hedge still on your right, at one stage passing a very strong, bench seat which, on closer inspection, turns out to be an old gatepost, complete with hinges. At the top of the incline, Stratford is revealed ahead.

The path now slants down again and, 60 yards after entering rough woodland and having passed the remains of a wartime shooting range in a dell on the left, turn left and continue to walk downhill. After a grassy portion, the well-trodden path goes left and right, passing an old gate and a path on the left, and soon resumes its former heading. After passing to the right of a large patch of Scots pine trees and to the left of a garden centre, a red-gravel drive leads to a road.

Here turn left and immediately pass Shottery St Andrews C. of E. Primary School. Built in 1870, its timber frame and intricate brick-and-stonework are noteworthy. At the next T-junction, go left, passing The Bell, and follow the road to a mini-roundabout. Cottage Lane is on your left and you walk down this to reach Anne Hathaway's Cottage.

Before her marriage to William Shakespeare in 1582, Anne Hathaway lived in this house which was occupied by the Hathaway family continuously from 1470 to 1911. The times of opening of the house and its surrounding gardens can be obtained by telephoning 01789 204016.

After visiting the house, cross the road and pass through a gate which leads over a footbridge and, turning right, onto Jubilee Walk which takes you back to the roundabout at the top of Cottage Lane. Take the road *opposite* Cottage Lane and embark on the track back into Stratford. At the bus stop in 30 yards, continue straight ahead along Tavern Lane (the sign is above

The Shakespeare Memorial in the Bancroft Gardens

eye-level on your left), with a garden centre also on your left. When the road swings right follow the green-and-white signposts initially to 'Stratford and Shakespeare's Birthplace' and subsequently to 'Old Town and Hall's Croft'.

If you have arrived by train you can, if you wish, take a shorter route back to the railway station by reading from ❂ below.

The path meanders between houses, past allotments and across playing fields and, although its signposts are relatively infrequent, the path is clear with no abrupt right or left turns. Finally emerging onto a main road (Evesham Place), go ahead into Chestnut Walk, turn left into Church Street, right into Chapel Lane (passing a yew topiary hedge behind which are beautiful gardens) and then left into Waterside at the end of which you reach your starting place.

❂ To return to the railway station turn left when you reach the playing fields and take the path signed 'Market Place, Shakespeare's Birthplace'. Go past a children's play area and a school. Reaching a road cross this, go left a few yards and turn right along the tarmacked footpath. At a Y-junction in the path turn right to reach Alcester Road where a left turn will bring you to the railway station.

20
Cleeve Prior, the Littletons and Marcliff

Explore pretty villages at the extreme east of Worcestershire with a very brief excursion into Warwickshire.

Start: The church of St Andrew, Cleeve Prior (GR088493) which is at the east end of the village.
Distance: 7½ miles; shorter option 5½ miles.
Maps: Landranger 150; Pathfinder 1020, 997.
Parking: Roadsides in Cleeve Prior.
Public Transport: MRW service 146 Birmingham/Evesham goes through Cleeve Prior.
Refreshments: The King's Arms in Cleeve Prior and the King Edward VII in South Littleton.

The historical records show that there was a church on this site in Cleeve Prior in 872, the nave of the present church dating from the thirteenth century and the chancel from the fourteenth. A delightful, hand-painted map of the district is on view within and the estimated age of the yew tree outside the south door is in excess of 600 years.

BY way of a metal kissing gate at its west end, leave the churchyard and walk 50 yards to the village green immediately turning left to pass between it and the Memorial Hall. The map in the church refers to an ancient elm on the green but this, like most of its relatives, must have succumbed to Dutch Elm Disease a few years ago. However, it is succeeded by the Jubilee beech (1935) and an oak, planted in 1992 to commemorate the fortieth year of the reign of Queen Elizabeth II.

Cross the road and enter Quarry Lane. Follow this, swinging gently to the right and, later, abruptly to the left, directed by a signpost to Middle Littleton. When the lane peters out near a pool, go ahead with the hedge on your left, the tower of Middle Littleton church coming into view ahead in the distance. When the hedge itself peters out, continue on the path ahead as it swings slightly to the right. Reaching a row of tall trees at the end of the field, turn right and walk for 20 yards, then cross a footbridge and stile on your left.

Ignoring a branch left, walk on more-or-less due south for about three-quarters of a mile with the fence initially on your right then on both sides and finally (now hedged) on your left, skirting to the west of North Littleton. On reaching a road, cross and proceed forward on the footpath directly opposite. At the end of the first field, cross a stile on your right and, with your back to this stile, make out a path leading half-left across the next field. Follow this path, noticing on your left a giant barn. Cross a stile and walk past houses for about 15 yards to a turn on your left which leads (passing a nice peacock weather vane) to Middle Littleton Tithe Barn. The entrance (not immediately visible) is to the left of the first large door to the barn.

Radio-carbon dating estimates that Middle Littleton Tithe Barn was built in 1260±30 years. Internally, it measures 136 feet by 32 feet. In the outbuilding nearest

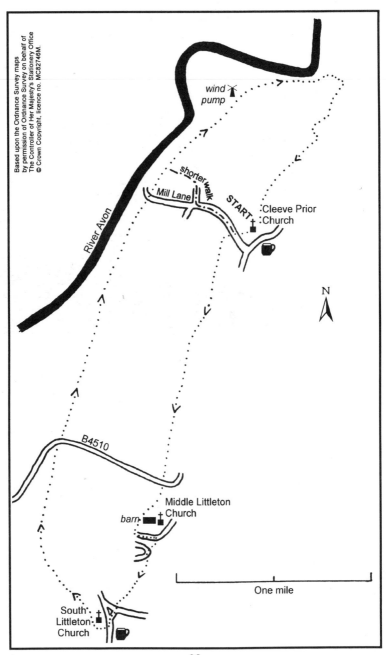

the church is a vertically-balanced millstone which, in grinding corn, used to roll round a circular track powered, presumably, by a horse. Taken over by the National Trust in 1975 in a dilapidated state, the barn has been sympathetically restored.

Having investigated the barn, retrace your steps to the houses in the lane and turn left to reach the main road through the village. Turn left and walk round to St Nicholas' church which has an impressively light interior, the only stained glass in its large windows being two small portions of ancient glass high up in its east window. The ancient yew in the churchyard hides much of the west end of the church.

The 700 year-old Tithe Barn at Middle Littleton

Leaving the church via its lych gate, cross the road and pass through a kissing gate opposite. Turn three-quarters right and proceed ahead beside power lines, soon to walk with a wire fence on your right. Pass through another kissing gate and, in a further 20 yards, yet another to reach a path between houses. On emerging onto a road, turn left and walk on for about 50 yards when, as the road continues to swing right, you fork to the left on a tarmacked path which ends with, inevitably, a kissing gate. Go through this and then walk half-right across the field ahead of you, noting the marked ridge-and-furrow pattern as you go.

At the far right-hand side of the field, this path merges with another to lead through (you guessed!) a kissing gate which leads to an enclosed path which delivers you onto a road. Walk straight ahead and, at the T-junction, turn left and walk to the fine old Manor House opposite the church. This listed building was built in 1721, complete with dormer windows and a turret with a 200-year-old weather-cock. Cross the road to the church of St Michael the Archangel.

Here is another church with features dating back to Norman times. Whilst admiring its antiquity, we must also respect the love and devotion with which members of these small communities maintain these fine old country churches in such pristine condition. How lucky we are!

Leaving the church by the south door, go straight ahead and pass through a metal gate which leads to a path onto which you turn right. After the gate at the end of this path, turn right through yet another kissing gate and walk ahead to reach Church Lane. Here, turn left to join a bridleway, initially passing in front of Church Farm. Follow this track north-west as it gradually ascends for nearly half a mile. At the top of the incline, just before four blue-and-white water board markers, turn right and, in 25 yards, veer left to reach a gate leading into Windmill Hill Nature Reserve.

Windmill Hill Nature Reserve is a six hectare Site of Special Scientific Interest and is maintained by the Worcestershire Wildlife Trust. It has wild orchids and twenty-nine species of butterflies have been recorded in it.

The bridleway follows the top of the escarpment but it can become very muddy. You may avoid this by making a detour through the Reserve on a path normally open to the public. However, if signs warn you that this path is closed, you should use the bridleway, however muddy. To go through the Reserve, 15 yards after the Reserve gate, cross a dilapidated stile on the left and walk on, parallel to the bridleway for another 15 yards when you take a path which slants down to the left with triple electricity cables overhead. Continue down this path, the green spire of Harvington church soon coming into view ahead – but not the Harvington which can be visited on Walk 3 in this book – with the River Avon in the foreground, meandering its way towards Evesham.

Cross a stile which leads to the path through the Reserve, parallel to, but about 50 yards down the escarpment from the bridleway. On this path, you cross three stiles (with dog-friendly gates beside them) and, after a fourth, you bear slightly right to rejoin the bridleway which leads to a road (B4510). (Shortly before the last stile, a conveniently-sited seat affords pleasant views over surrounding countryside.)

Cross this road and turn right. Walk on for 30 yards and, just beyond a house, turn left to rejoin the bridleway at the head of the escarpment. After a quarter of a mile or so, Cleeve Prior comes into view ahead and to the right. Stay on this path, as it follows the top of Cleeve Hill, for about a mile when the vegetation on the left opens up to provide more good views to the west, and you may choose to enjoy them from another well-placed bench seat. Continue ahead for a further 600 yards when you reach a lane, Mill Lane. Cross this lane and continue on the bridleway (signposted to Marlcliff). In about 125 yards, you pass a cottage and, in a further 100 yards, you reach, straddling the lane, a farm gate with a wicket gate beside it.

*Here the two routes diverge. For the **shorter** route continue from the following paragraph. For the **longer** walk continue from ★ below.*

Turn right just before the gates and walk ahead with the field boundary on your right. At the end of the field, bear slightly right to join a lane (Nightingale Lane) and follow this as it swings to the right. Then take the first left turn and then the first right to enter Froglands Lane which soon leads to Cleeve Prior's pretty, main street into which you turn left to return to your starting place.

★ Following the **longer** route, continue through the gate and follow the lane until it ends by a Cotswold-stone house. Walk ahead and pass through a wicket gate still following the bridleway. You will see two churches – one ahead , at Bidford-on-Avon (in Warwickshire) and the other on your left, at Salford Priors (in Worcestershire). When the enclosed path ends, continue on a rough cinder track with the wire fence on your left, soon to pass a corroded wind pump which would have been ideally-suited to this exposed spot. The path, soon approaches the Avon again. High hedges obscure it initially (you may hear the sound of one of its weirs down to your left) but, soon after it comes into view, its course changes, flowing towards you from the north as you cross the county boundary. Pass through two wicket gates and walk through a strip of pasture land to reach a metal-covered, wooden seat.

If you are travelling by bus and find yourself pressed for time, you might wish to shorten your walk to finish in Marlcliff. In this case fork left down a grassy bank towards a white-walled, thatched cottage just before which, gates lead to the road into the village.

Otherwise, stay on the high ground and walk on for about 100 yards where you cross a stile on your right. Walk up the field, bearing very slightly right, to a stile. Having crossed this, bear very slightly left to climb over your next stile. Continue ahead on a well-trodden path across the next field, soon flanking an old apple orchard. After the orchard, pass through a gap in the hedge, turn left and walk round the edge of the field with the hedge on your left.

Fifteen yards after passing the second corner of this field, cross a stile and continue on the clear path, aiming to the right of the larger clump of tall trees ahead. The path gradually swings left, passing a small pool and crossing a footbridge. Beyond this, you pass to the right of Cleeve Prior's Manor House, noticing the round dovecote in its grounds. Beneath a splendid horse chestnut and through a row of thirty-one proud poplars, you enter the churchyard having completed the circuit.

Index

Also from Meridian…

COUNTRY WALKS IN WARWICKSHIRE AND WORCESTERSHIRE
by Des Wright

Twenty circular walks that explore some of the two counties most attractive areas. The walking is easy, mostly on the flat and with few climbs. Distances range from 2½ to 8½ miles although some can be combined to give longer walks. ISBN 1 869922 33 6. £5.95. 96 pages. 16 photographs. 21 maps.

WALKS TO WET YOUR WHISTLE
by Roger Seedhouse

Eighteen walks covering some of the most beautiful countryside in Shropshire and along its Staffordshire borders, each providing an opportunity to visit a pub in which the walker will feel welcome and comfortable. The main walks range in distance between 7 and 11½ miles but each has a shorter alternative of between 2¾ and 5¼ miles. ISBN 1 869922 34 4. £5.95. 112 pages. 17 photographs. 18 maps.

WALKS AROUND THE MALVERNS
by Roy Woodcock

The Malvern Hills and their surroundings provide magnificent opportunities for rambling and the twenty walks in this book cover the entire range of hills and the neighbouring commons, together with some of the delightful countryside nearby. Distances range from two miles to eight miles, plus a leg stretcher of between ten and sixteen miles (depending on the starting point) that takes in the full length of the ridge and ascends all the Malvern peaks. ISBN 1 869922 32 8. £5.95. 112 pages. 32 illustrations. 20 maps.

MORE WATERSIDE WALKS IN THE MIDLANDS
by Birmingham Ramblers: edited by Peter Groves

Following on the success of their first book, *Waterside Walks in the Midlands*, members of the City of Birmingham Branch of the Ramblers' Association have now prepared another collection on a similar theme. As before, the walks feature brooks, streams, rivers, canals and pools - sometimes as a major aspect of a walk, sometimes as a feature to encounter as you ramble through some of the fine Midlands countryside. Distances range from 4½ miles to14 miles. ISBN 1 869922 31 X. £5.95 112 pages. 21 photographs. 18 maps. Paperback. A5.

FAVOURITE WALKS IN THE WEST MIDLANDS
by members of the Birmingham CHA Rambling Club,
Edited by Tom Birch and Mary Wall

A collection of twenty-two attractive walks from members of one of Birmingham's oldest walking clubs. Most have shorter and longrer alternatives, the shorter walks ranging from 5½ to 7½ miles, the longer walks from 7 to 10 miles. ISBN 1 869922 26 3. £4.95. 112 pages. 24 photographs. 23 maps.

All Meridian titles are available from booksellers or, if in difficulty, direct from the publishers. Please send your remittance, including the following amounts for postage and packing:
Order value up to £5.00 add 75p; up to £10.00 add £1.00; over £10.00 add £1.50.

Meridian Books • 40 Hadzor Road • Oldbury • B68 9LA
Prices correct January 1999
Please write for our complete catalogue